The **M**-factor
Media confidence *for* **business leaders** *and* **managers**

The M FACTOR

Media confidence *for*
business leaders *and* **managers**

TOM MADDOCKS

The **M**-factor
Media confidence *for* **business leaders** *and* **managers**

First published in 2013 by
Anoma Press Ltd
48 St Vincent Drive, St Albans, Herts, AL1 5SJ UK

info@anomapress.com
www.anomapress.com

Cartoons by Roger Leboff
Author photo by Ivan Bellaroba
Cover design by Michael Inns
Artwork by Karen Gladwell

Printed on acid-free paper from managed forests.
This book is printed on demand to fulfill orders,
so no copies will be remaindered or pulped.

Printed and bound by TJ International Ltd, Padstow, Cornwall

ISBN 978-1-908746-72-6

Contents

FACTOR

Acknowledgements

My thanks are due to all the people who have inspired me and educated me, both in journalism and after – far too many to remember, let alone list. Particular appreciation is reserved, however, for those who took the time to comment on and help improve early manuscripts: Fiona Harris, Jamie Jago, Simon Goldie, Vee Montebello, Amanda Chick, Anne Read and Liz Wood. All efforts underpinned, as ever, by the patience and support of Anne and George.

FACTOR

Foreword

Whether we like it or not, the press, radio and television exert a huge influence on all of us. Add to these forces the growing power of social media, and it becomes even more important for every organisation to think clearly about how it communicates its message. More than ever, business leaders need to show they are able to embrace media opportunities, as well as deal with the challenges. The basics of how to prepare, handle, anticipate old fashioned questions from old fashioned reporters very much still apply.

At last, then, here is a common-sense, modern book to show how the Chief Executive or manager can work with the media, rather than see only a potential threat. Tom Maddocks has turned his skills and time as a journalist into becoming one of the best media trainers in the business. I am amazed he is sharing all of his secrets, but don't argue with it, read it!

Julia Hobsbawm
Founder and CEO, Editorial Intelligence
Hon. Visiting Professor in Networking, Cass Business School

Introduction
The M-factor

Who wins The X Factor or any other television talent show? The winner isn't usually the person who just possesses raw, indefinable talent. Application is required, as well as a feel for what will go down well with the public, and an element of surprise and charm.

What I call the M-factor is about being at ease with the media: delivering what reporters and editors are looking for, and knowing how to use press, radio and television opportunities to your advantage. The M-factor, too, is something that a few people seem to be born with, while most of the rest of us have to work at possessing it. Not everyone can become a media star. But, with practice - and the help of this book - the great majority of managers, entrepreneurs and CEOs can not only get the M-factor, but benefit greatly from it.

In the course of interviewing many hundreds of people during my twenty-odd years as a news reporter and business journalist, I came to realise how difficult lots of people in business and public sector bodies find dealing with the media. Some individuals are media naturals. But others are much more afraid of being misquoted, or misrepresented in print and of making mistakes and coming over poorly in a radio or television interview. These concerns mean that they cannot see the upside of being able to acquire the skills to make use of the media to sell their products, or to raise their profile, to make their voice heard and to help set the agenda. Social media fills these individuals with an equal amount of dread which also stops them exploiting the promotional opportunities on offer.

Avoiding media opportunities puts organisations at a huge disadvantage, not only missing opportunities to position themselves in a favourable light when they have done something good, and less able to make their arguments heard when there is debate about their industry or their future, but typically leading to defensiveness when under criticism or even attack. M-factor organisations are generally seen in a better light by the public, have their views taken more seriously by those that matter, have a higher profile for their products and services, and can deal more effectively with a crisis. This book tries to address all those concerns, and provide practical solutions; it is designed to be read right through from cover to cover or to be dipped into when needed.

So, what is the M-factor? M, of course, stands for media, but the M-factor is not about you trying to take on the media and coming out the winner: it is more about partnership – you understanding what reporters and editors are looking for, and where possible being able to deliver it, to the benefit of both sides. It is about you feeling as comfortable as one of those media naturals in working with press, online, radio and television journalists, feeling that you instinctively know what is likely to interest them, when it is right to engage, and when it is perhaps a good time to pull back. It is about being able to realistically deal with tricky issues, rather than be evasive or defensive. Above all, it is about seeing the journalist as someone who is more likely to provide an opportunity than a threat, someone it is worth trying to get to know and understand.

You do not have to become a full-blown "media tart", constantly seeking the next headline; that is not what getting the M-factor is about. This is about taking the right media opportunities at the right time, and making them work to the benefit of you and your organisation. For people in the corporate world, there are two broad categories of opportunity. The first comes when you create your own story, such as with a new product launch or event. The second comes when you raise your profile by commenting on external events in your field of expertise – new legislation, industry trends, economic data and so on. As we shall discover, these opportunities can be found across the range of traditional and new media – as can the threats, if your organisation hits trouble.

There are many advantages in acquiring the M-factor, and to do so is not nearly as hard as you may imagine.

Having the M-factor

If you....

- *see the media as a vital opportunity to raise profile, increase brand awareness, and set the agenda*

- *usually look forward to a reporter's call, rather than fear it*

- *easily get a good feel for what the story is and what the journalist is looking for*

- *try hard to have something interesting to say, so it has been worth the reporter's time*

- *generally get your point across, without being pushy or glib*

- *can speak in clear language, not business jargon*

- *can usually judge when it is right to engage with the media, and when not*

- *make the effort to perform well on radio or television, with plenty of energy*

- *know where to look and how to sit so that you appear comfortable on television*

- *can keep your cool in a tough interview rather than getting angry or running for the hills*

- *try as hard as possible to answer the question, not avoid it*

... then you truly have the M-factor.

Chapter 1

Business benefits from smart use of the media

The right media mix will benefit your business

Business benefits from smart use of the media

Newspapers, magazines, news websites, television and radio – the "mass media" – are consumed by billions of people every day around the world. They are the most powerful ways ever devised to communicate with large numbers of people. If you have a message to get across, a product to sell or people you wish to influence, why on earth would you not want to take best advantage of the opportunities they provide to reach these massive audiences?

Yet many organisations are wary to say the least. They fear reporters will misunderstand them, or want to write bad things about them, or they may believe they have nothing of interest to say. They imagine that entrepreneurs and business leaders such as Sir Richard Branson, Donald Trump and the *Dragons' Den* entrepreneurs who frequently appear on television or in the papers do it only for ego reasons, and are too keen on the sight of their own name in print and the sound of their own voices. If you are one of these, my message to you is: Yes, there is a "threat" side to the media – and you would be foolish to ignore it – but do not let the "threat" side blind you to the "opportunity" side.

Let's begin with the top five reasons for lack of participation given to me by chief executives and managers who have been reluctant to get involved with the media, and examine whether their arguments stand up.

1 I'm too busy

All chief executives and senior managers are busy people – of course they are. There are challenging markets to conquer, strategies to formulate, projects to complete, stakeholders to placate. However, contributing to editorial copy in newspapers and making authoritative radio and television appearances can be a vital component of the overall marketing mix, raising the profile of the company as a leading player in its market. Experience with the more positive side of the media will also help equip you with the skills to deal effectively with any trickier issues that might arise.

2 I might get misquoted or misunderstood

Many executives I meet hate the fact that they cannot really control what journalists write – this makes media interviews too risky in their view, especially if they are engaged in any activity as a company that is not universally popular, such as banking. However, there are many easy steps you can take to reduce (although not eliminate) the risk, which we will cover in subsequent chapters.

It is true that journalists, being human beings, are far from perfect; they may get things wrong – more likely through genuine error than malign intent. Reporters are also likely to speak to several sources, and in the process obtain contrasting views of what happened in a particular situation; there is rarely just one view of the truth. The finished article may reflect these alternative perspectives even if they do not sit easily with your own. The best advice I can give here is "don't sweat the small stuff" – get a sense of perspective. I frequently hear of executives who get incredibly angry over a single article about them that gets something wrong, forgetting about the positive publicity they have had from ten other articles that were broadly accurate. Small errors may seem important to you but will usually go unnoticed to the great majority of readers, and are unlikely to sway their opinion of your organisation so long as the general gist is fair and accurate. If there are serious factual errors then you have recourse to take this up with the publication, for instance with a "Letter to the Editor", correcting the facts and bringing forward some positive points.

3   Reporters are only interested in bad news

Of course, conflict makes a much better story than benign collaboration. Newspapers need to sell copies so they naturally put the most dramatic stories – 'crisis', 'shock', 'drama', etc – on the front pages. This is pretty much in line with readers' expectations. Take the transport system as an example: If things are running normally then people do not want to waste their time reading about it; however, if the system has broken down in some way, and if there has been a train crash with people injured, readers expect to see lots of coverage, with pictures. So in that sense bad news sells. But readers would soon tire if every page was a parade of misery. The tabloids have plenty of human interest and celebrity features, and if you look at the more serious newspapers, most of the stories on the inside pages are much more of an everyday mix of good and bad, depending on your perspective: "UK border checks to be tightened", "Sony in deal with JK Rowling", "Metro strike *talks fail". Many stories – product launches, profile pieces and so on – are very much public relations (PR)-led. An interesting exercise is to look through the key industry publications that your current or potential customers or clients might read, and estimate the percentage that present comment opportunities, are relatively even-handed, are benign, or are promotional in their content. By and large, industry publications cannot afford to focus only on mudslinging; to do so would mean that they would not be taken seriously and that they would soon run out of people willing to deal with them.*

4 I might make a mess of it if I am interviewed on radio or television, and look stupid

It's true, you might. But I usually find that, when I meet a CEO for media coaching, or a group of executives, there is an enormous amount that can be done to boost confidence and to prepare them to grab the opportunities. Effective preparation is key to ensuring that you are ready and rehearsed with some powerful points to put across. As they say: Fail to prepare? Prepare to fail.

5 Other people within the organisation could do it better than me, so I should leave it to them

Again, it's possible. Yet most of the "media-savvy" people I meet started out as lacking in confidence with dealing with the media as the next man or woman. From my experience, there are roughly 10% at the top who are media naturals, who seem to instinctively know what's needed, and love it. They already have the M-factor. Another 10% at the bottom will never be really comfortable in the media spotlight. But with the other 80%, effective coaching can make a huge difference, particularly with regular practice to keep the skills fresh.

The media as a megaphone

I liken the media to a megaphone, which is sitting on the table in front of you. You are reluctant to pick it up and start using it, for fear that people won't like what you have to say – perhaps they will want to throw rotten fruit at you. So you leave it on the table for the time being. Sooner or later, however, someone else will walk by, and be amazed you aren't making use of it. So they pick it up themselves and start shouting their message through it. They draw a crowd, and you are left on the sidelines thinking, "Why on earth didn't I do that? I know much more about this subject than that person does. Why isn't it me that they are listening to?" It's worth remembering that if a reporter is looking for a comment from you, and you won't give them one, they will probably go straight to your nearest competitor. So you have effectively handed the opportunity to them on a plate.

As I have said, I am not suggesting that you should try to turn yourself into a media tart – the kind of person who will make themselves available at the drop of a hat, 24/7, in the hope of getting their name in the paper or their voice on the radio. There may be people in your own industry sector who you see quoted so regularly that your instinctive reaction is, "Oh no, not him again." It is best to be available, but not *too* available. You do not want to fall into the trap of becoming a rent-a-quote.

To get the M-factor, be strategic. Your media strategy should be led by the business strategy of your organisation. Think about the groups you really want to influence, and how the right media profile could help you reach those audiences. Should you be using the trade press, local papers or the nationals to communicate with particular stakeholders – regulators, parliamentary committees or local authorities – as well as potential customers and clients?

What signals do you want to send? Do you want to position yourself in the market as a young, brash challenger brand or as a long-established "natural choice" for those who see quality as being more important than price? Your choice of media and the style and tone you adopt can all reinforce these images and impressions. What are the main strengths in what you offer? What differentiates you from your competition? You can use every media interview as an opportunity to get these points across. Don't be afraid to repeat messages when you speak to journalists – even if they do not appear in the finished article or broadcast interview, your positioning will be much clearer to the reporters, who may be highly influential in their field. They are more likely to describe your company and its positioning accurately, and they will know better when the right times are to contact you for comment in the future.

The media can really come into their own when you have a new product or service to sell. A large part of the commercial success of many of the world's most successful companies has been through high-profile media coverage. Think of the millions of words that are written in publications around the globe every time that Microsoft launches a new version of Windows, analysing the details of each feature. Supplemented by advertising campaigns, this means nearly everyone in nearly every country is aware of the event.

Perhaps the extreme example is Apple. It has had an obsessive following for years because of its innovative and beautifully designed products. The company has played on its culture of secrecy to turn each product launch into a media event. During his lifetime the mental image of Steve Jobs, dressed in his black turtleneck top and blue jeans at one of those big events in San Francisco became an increasingly familiar one, with a giant screen above his head showing the latest shiny, desirable object – iPod, iPhone, iPad and so on. The day after, those pictures appeared in most of the world's leading newspapers, typically on the front page, as well as on all the television news channels. Then, once the product became available in the stores, those same papers and news bulletins would cover the queues of people waiting at the Apple Store to get their hands on one. Without spending a penny on advertising, the whole world had been made aware of the new device, and many of its key features. It is impossible to measure the 'dollar value' of such coverage, but globally it probably runs into the billions.

In the UK, Sir Richard Branson is another extreme example. He built his name by ensuring that the media had plenty of angles and always wanted to see what he was up to. Unlike many people, he was unafraid to be controversial and to criticise his competitors, making himself suitably quote-worthy. Another of his techniques has been to ensure there is always a good picture to grab the editor's and readers' attention – Branson dressed in a funny outfit, surrounded by a bevy of pretty girls, taking part in some sort of stunt. This of course is not to everyone's taste – again, it depends on brand and positioning. But over the years it has saved his companies millions in the advertising that would otherwise have been needed to build up brand awareness. At the last count, his companies employed 50,000 people across the globe with turnover approximately £13bn.

There are hundreds of more everyday examples, too. One organisation I worked with in the financial sector managed to achieve some positive media coverage in the Saturday personal finance sections, for a new fund it was launching. The following Monday, its call centres reported hundreds of additional enquiries requesting information about the product, most of whom, when asked, saying that they saw the article in the paper.

Another organisation had made some modest upgrades to the functionality of its software platform, which was reported in a couple of fairly obscure trade journals. One of those articles was seen by a potential client in North America that had for years been unsuccessfully targeted by the company in question. Now these people were on the phone asking for a meeting to talk about the platform and what it could do for them. They turned into a long-term customer, worth hundreds of thousands of pounds a year in additional revenue.

Smaller organisations often find it a tougher challenge to get media coverage because they do not have a well-known brand name, so there is little interest in their story. There is a chicken-and-egg element here – the better known you become, the more the media are interested, so you get more coverage and become still better known. So you have to work rather harder to go out to the media at the early stages, as they are unlikely to be coming to you. A smart PR, either internal or an external agency, is invaluable at this point, and you do have to be patient. It helps that journalists often copy one another. If a new name starts cropping up in one publication, others start to spot this and wonder if they're missing out or are falling behind the curve, so you may find that rival publications start calling you too, in the hope of interesting material. In addition, always remember that the specialist correspondents on the national newspapers read the trade publications in the areas they are covering, so your name may come to their attention sooner or later.

Another client I have worked with at this level is clear about its strategy – it is eyeing an IPO (Initial Public Offering – or stockmarket float) at some point in the future, and needs to get its name out there to build awareness among potential investors. Again, the expectation is that there will be a clear relationship between media exposure and future shareholder value.

You can set the agenda

It is remarkable how a memorable quote in the right place can establish you as an authority on your topic, or a leader in your field rather than a follower. This may be much more useful to you than overtly trying to shout from the rooftops about your latest computer, equity fund or air route. People tend to see an appearance in a well-regarded publication as a stamp of quality – otherwise that publication would have gone to somebody else. People take editorial copy much more seriously than advertising, as it is seen as being much more objective.

Many organisations, for example in consultancy and financial services, want to position themselves as the experts in their field; in the jargon, they would like to see themselves as "thought leaders". This, of course, is helpful for attracting new customers. For instance, suppose you are looking for a new mortgage, and you are faced with a choice of three mortgage brokers. You have never heard of two of the firms, but the boss of the third has the M-factor – he is a familiar name from regular articles on the subject. You have no idea if the unknown firms are cowboys or not; however, you are fairly sure the third is well respected, otherwise the papers would not be regularly quoting its views. You are much more likely to become a customer of the third.

There may be legislative or regulatory changes afoot that will affect your business. A good relationship with the key journalists in the field should make it much easier to get them interested in the changes and see the issues from your point of view. If you have frequently helped them out in the past, they are likely to already be 'on-side'. Again, smaller but more media-friendly organisations can punch above their weight. If comment is required on an industry issue, and the deadline is looming, reporters will turn immediately to the people they already know and trust. You want this to be you, so that it is your message and your agenda that is being reported, not the opposition's.

In short, an appropriate media profile, with some good media contacts, can make you a more valuable asset to your organisation.

In good times and bad

Of course it is rarely all smooth sailing in business, and larger, high-profile organisations can find the media spotlight extremely uncomfortable when they hit tough times. This is the point at which it is too late to try to build good media relationships – you are already in trouble in one way or another. The controversial investment bank Goldman Sachs is a good example. Enormously powerful and highly successful, Goldman Sachs was seen as being extremely arrogant by the media during the boom years. It created the impression it was 'above all that sort of thing', and was rarely helpful when returning journalists' calls. That meant that when the investment banks had a near-death experience in 2008 at the time of the collapse of Lehman Brothers, it had few media friends it could call on. The publicity when the bank's bosses were hauled in front of US Senators in 2010 to explain some of their actions was horrendous; Goldman-bashing had become everybody's favoured sport.

Some belated attempts to curry media favour backfired, because by that time editors and reporters had made up their minds about the story – it was never going to be turned round into a "these millionaire bankers are actually good guys, you know" angle. These guys were instead firmly entrenched in the public mind as the villains, and any publication that sought to go against the flow would look silly, or as if they were in the bank's pocket. The most notorious episode was CEO Lloyd Blankfein's quote to *The Sunday Times*, when he apparently claimed, *"we're only doing God's work."* Doubtless this was meant as a throwaway, flippant remark, but the damage was done. It reverberated around the world and has been used against Goldmans ever since. Had Mr Blankfein been more used to dealing with the media, I am sure he would not have made such an error in not thinking about how his words would look as a newspaper headline.

I am not trying to suggest that bonus-toting bankers would have won popularity contests if only their PR had been better – far from it. The media needs heroes and villains, and the likes of banks and big oil companies are rarely going to be found in the former category. However, they should not be surprised if their side of the story goes unheard if they tend only to offer up "no comment" or its equivalent to the media. No organisation, of course, should expect sympathetic coverage if its people are flouting regulations or breaking the law; that is not what the M-factor is about. This is about the many thousands of companies and other bodies that are trying to do the best job they can in sometimes difficult circumstances, who want to know how they can work with the media in as positive a way as possible, with any luck to mutual benefit.

Companies that take an M-factor approach still get into trouble, and still get criticised by the media when they do; however, the impact is usually much less severe. Unlike many high-profile companies, many of Sir Richard Branson's businesses have failed (Virgin Cola, Virgin Cars, Virgin Clothing, or Virgin Brides, anyone?). But because of his assiduously cultivated media relationships, coverage of these difficult episodes has been relatively muted, with much more attention paid to the latest big deal or photo-opportunity. Again, you do not have to go to extremes, but there is a lesson to be learned here. Build up strong media relationships in the good times and they will help you in the bad.

Key Reminders

■ *Many people have a defensive attitude regarding
the media but there are plenty of business benefits
to creating good relationships with journalists –
see the opportunities, not just the threats.
Successful companies can be rewarded by huge
financial payback if they can achieve positive coverage.*

■ *You cannot control what a journalist will write but
there are steps you can take to reduce the risk of
something going wrong. Mistakes can and do occur
but they are not necessarily damaging to your
business – don't worry about minor details.*

■ *Editors get excited by drama and conflict but not all
publications have a tabloid agenda. The business
and trade press carry a mix of items, and there are
many positive as well as negative stories.*

■ *Almost everyone can massively improve their
confidence and ability to perform on radio and
television with the right coaching, and practice.*

■ *Let your media strategy be led by the business
strategy of your organisation. Work out which
audiences you need to influence and prepare
appropriate messages to enable you to set the
right agenda.*

■ *Get comfortable in dealing with journalists when
you have the opportunity, so you understand their
requirements. Do not leave it until times of crisis
– by then it will be too late.*

Chapter 2

Understanding the media mindset

*To build a good relationship with journalists
you need to understand how they think*

FACTOR

Understanding the media mindset

The better you become at understanding the mindset of the journalist, the easier it will be to deliver what journalists want, to foresee the tricky angles, and to progress towards the M-factor. Like any trade or profession, the personality types will vary considerably, but there are characteristics that crop up more often than not. Radio and television presenters and reporters deliver their material in a very different style from those purely working with words on a page or screen; for the specifics on how to deal with appearing on television and radio, see chapters 9 and 10. The mindset and approach of broadcast journalists, however, tends to be very similar to those of 'print' journalists; many have worked across the media. So most of the following points apply to anyone you may come across from radio or television, as well as those dealing in the written word.

What type of person are you dealing with?

Reporters tend to be under a lot of pressure. Their environment is highly competitive, and those working in hard news live in constant fear of 'missing the story'. It is not just the nationals or the television news channels that take this extremely seriously. Trade publications closely compare themselves to rivals and the reporter who regularly has weaker quotes and a less compelling angle than the competition can expect a kicking from the editor. This means that they may frequently appear impatient, and when under particular stress this can sometimes veer into unpleasantness. Most, however, tend to find that they achieve more by charm than by bullying.

Broadcast journalists in particular see it as their role to be provocative and to play devil's advocate in their interviews. Questions such as, "Your last product was a disastrous failure, why on earth do you think this one is going to do any better?", do not necessarily mean that the reporter hates you, although it may feel like that at the time. It is more likely that the journalist wants to demonstrate to the world that they have given you a good grilling and they are not just an arm of your PR machine. If you give a good solid answer, they will respect you and usually move on to the next question..

Typically reporters are not very well paid – one of the reasons so many leave newspapers for the world of PR. They are more likely to be desk-bound nowadays, interviewing contacts by telephone rather than winkling out stories over long lunches. Their attitude is likely to be one that questions authority. However, in my experience they are highly susceptible to flattery. If you tell them you enjoy their publication and always read their column (this has to have truth in it, of course, otherwise you will soon be found out), they can become your friend for life.

They are driven by deadlines, which typically used to come once a day or once a week, but which for many are now continuous, with increasing pressure to get stories on to their publication's website. So the contact who doesn't respond to a journalist's query until some hours later is unlikely to build a lasting relationship with them. Much better to give a high priority to media enquiries, then you will become the one whose name comes to mind when they are up against it. If you scratch their back, they may well be in a position to scratch yours one day. Try to build up a good long-term relationship with the key journalists in your area. Be aware of their deadlines, so you know when they are under most time pressure. When trust has been built, they can also be a good source of intelligence and information about your market; after all, they are meeting with your peers and competitors.

In terms of their skills, some reporters earn a reputation as 'story-getters' but their words need to be heavily rewritten in order to read well and look good on the page. Others are no good at hard news, but play to different strengths, for instance the ability to turn out a beautifully crafted 1,500-word feature piece at extremely high speed. The best publications have a blend of these different types.

Journalists frequently fail to take what they have been told at face value, and this can be a source of friction with people they interview. I have often worked with company bosses and managers who feel that what is written as the result of a conversation fails to reflect what was actually said. Sometimes this is slipshod journalism; other times, it is simply that the reporter has spoken to other contributors who see the issue from a different perspective. Reporters have to try to work out where the truth lies; they certainly do not see it as their role simply to act as the faithful scribe who always trots out the corporate line – that is just advertising.

Much has been written about the culture of 'spin' in recent years, with politicians and big business putting the best possible gloss on the facts in an effort to control how stories are covered in the press and on radio and television. Political party spin doctors have in some cases become almost as well known as the politicians themselves. This has arisen from the understandable aim to ensure that politicians' messages come over clearly and fairly through the media, but the depressing by-product is that both print and broadcast journalists are nowadays far more suspicious of what they are told by big organisations of all types, and are often frustrated by the layers of communications experts there to protect their senior people. They have been 'spun to' too often in the past, and in some cases this could more accurately be described as 'lied to'.

My advice is not to try to be too clever with 'spinning'. If you are perceived by journalists as having misled them, any trust that had been built up is likely to be lost and will probably never be recovered, by you or your organisation as a whole. Stick to the truth. Make what you say clear and unambiguous, and do not be afraid to repeat your message. You will rarely if ever be in a position to tell the whole truth, as with nearly every organisation there will be information that is not in the public domain, but what you do say should be accurate; if there are specific areas you cannot go into, try where possible to explain why.

Another frequent remark I hear from executives who deal with reporters from time to time is, "I was surprised at how little he/she knew about the subject." They find themselves having to explain what they see as the basics on the topic, and are fearful that they will be misrepresented if the reporter hasn't really understood what they are trying to say.

In fact some journalists are extremely knowledgeable, with in-depth expertise built up over many years and a thick book full of industry contacts. They may know a lot more about some aspects of your sector than you do. However, others will be less knowledgeable, less smart. Newspaper and magazine journalists have to cover a wide range of topics and cannot be expert in all of them. However, when there are gaps in their understanding they do not always like to admit it. So do not assume knowledge; avoid industry jargon and offer to help them with background information. If you sense they are floundering on a technical topic, use a phrase such as, "I know a lot of people find this area confusing, would it help if I explain the background?" You can then give the necessary context without being patronising, saving the reporter from the embarrassment of admitting they do not know something they suspect they ought to.

Deep down most journalists take great pride in what they do. They want to get information fast but they want it to be accurate – contrary to popular opinion, a reporter on any remotely serious publication who consistently gets his or her facts wrong is likely to be shown the door. There may still be tabloid journalists who operate on the basis of "never let the facts get in the way of a good story" but following the Leveson Inquiry, UK newspapers now face rather tougher regulation, and editors have gradually become more accountable. Most big corporate organisations rarely deal with tabloids, which tend to be much more interested in celebrity gossip and football rather than the humdrum world the majority of companies inhabit. If you do find yourself in the tabloids' line of sight, for example, if they have had reader complaints about your product or service, your best response as an organisation is to treat them with respect and tell it straight; do not underestimate them.

What is "news"?

Some definitions of news...

"News is what somebody, somewhere wants to suppress. All the rest is advertising."

- Lord Northcliffe, founder of the Daily Mail

"News is the first rough draft of history."

—Ben Bradlee, former editor of The Washington Post

"News is people. It is people talking and people doing."

- Harry Evans, former editor of The Sunday Times

Bad news isn't everything

Newspaper editors are looking for timely content that is of relevance and interest to their readers – it is as simple as that. Your job, if you want to build up that good relationship with them, is to provide some of that content. The more you understand how they think, the more likely you are to be able to deliver the sort of thing they are looking for. Sometimes you will have a story for them; if you are trying to interest them in something your business is doing, look at it from the perspective of how it will affect their readers – rather than just from your own point of view. Otherwise, why should they care?

See if you can find what journalists call a 'peg' – a reason for them to write the story today, rather than last week or next month. This makes it easier for them to "sell" the idea to their editors. It could be linked to the impact of a new piece of legislation about to come into force, or the forthcoming budget, or perhaps the anniversary of some relevant event – anything to give your topic some pertinence or urgency. The more serious publications are looking for something that is of significance to their readers; those at the more populist end often focus as much on stories that may not be significant at all – celebrity or industry gossip, for instance – but will make a lively and entertaining read. Either way, something counterintuitive, something a little bit surprising, will always be more likely to catch editors' attention – aim for something that won't just make them think to themselves, "Oh well, they would say that, wouldn't they." Think about the key publications in your sector, and what types of stories they typically cover, to increase your chances of hitting the target.

On other occasions, the reporter already has a story, and is just looking for reaction from someone well placed to comment. In this situation there is probably a choice of who to approach, so you are in a competitive market for quotes – you often need them more than they need you. In many senses, it is a business relationship.

You have what they want in terms of views, quotes and information, while they have what you want – access to their audiences, which could run into thousands, tens of thousands, or even millions of people. So how does that fit in with the day-to-day perception that the papers only contain news of scandal and disaster?

Papers naturally put dramatic, eye-catching stories on the front page when they can – after all, they need to sell as many copies as possible to survive. Stories of conflict and outrage tend to fit the bill. As I have mentioned, news is frequently created when the system breaks down. So a headline reading "Train service runs as usual" would not capture your attention, but "Train crash kills twenty" would. "Little action on stock market" v "Stocks crash in market panic"? You know which you would be more likely to read. However, good news such as the occasional England football victory will also make the front page, as will the cheering picture story about a small child being rescued from drowning, or the national set-piece event such as a royal wedding. After the Queen's 2012 Diamond Jubilee celebrations (on every front page bar one, in some cases for several days on end) *The Times* printed a special "wraparound" picture supplement that added 100,000 to circulation on the day it came out. Other papers have similar stories to tell; during the subsequent London Olympic and Paralympic Games, nearly every title was dominated by positive Team GB gold medal stories for what seemed like weeks on end.

A lot of the material on the inside pages is much less dramatic, but nonetheless still of relevance and interest to the readers, or at least some of them. Political stories are often hyped up into big shouting matches to add some conflict and make them more eye-catching, but much of the material is simply factual, for example, about new plans and proposals, everything from the new high-speed rail link, to changes in the school exam system, which may be a mixture of good and bad news, depending on which side of the argument you sit.

A remarkable chunk of what appears in newspapers and magazines in all parts of the world is actually PR-generated, particularly when you think of all the supplements covering style, personal finance, motoring, travel and so on. The same applies to television and radio. The editor of the UK edition of *GQ* has admitted that many of the ideas in the publication come from his PR contacts – and he is just being more honest than most. Research on this was carried out by Cardiff University for the 2008 book *Flat Earth News* by *The Guardian*'s journalist Nick Davies, who levelled criticism at the rise of "churnalism" in the UK. The research suggested that 80% of 2,000 stories surveyed from five leading UK national newspapers were wholly or partly constructed from second hand material provided by news agencies or press releases, rather than being researched by reporters.

Partly this is a reflection of the fact that journalists are not so much lazy as overworked, as publications have reduced editorial teams as pressure on budgets has grown. Typically there are fewer reporters having to write more articles than in the past, and there is enormous pressure for them to get material online before somebody else does – this will inevitably lead to shortcuts and inaccuracies. More than ever, PR firms are becoming content creators – ideal for those papers (all of them) with websites with an infinite amount of space to fill.

The seven interview types

So how might your interaction with the media work? For most people it will usually be by telephone rather than face to face. Radio interviews are frequently carried out this way. Sometimes reporters – particularly from trade or technical publications – will not bother to speak to you at all, simply emailing a list of questions and expecting you to sit down and spend lots of time crafting careful answers to each one. They can then cut and paste the bits they like into their finished article, essentially getting you to do most of the work for them. Of course, having written their email, they can easily send it to five other people as well, all of whom are also expected to dance to the reporter's tune. I see this as a depressing trend, and a very lazy form of journalism. Of course it means you can choose your words exactly when being quoted, but generally I would not devote a lot of time to this. If you are busy, just jot down a few paragraphs outlining the main points you wish to make – or simply ask them to give you a call.

Otherwise, I would argue that the vast majority of media interviews fall into one of seven categories, and these can make a big difference to the way you are portrayed in the final article, so it is well worth finding out before you speak to a reporter quite where you fit in.

▼ Expert commentator/pundit

This type of interview is extremely common. Every time something happens – the latest house price index is released, there's a terrorist alert, Microsoft issues some new software – there are gaping holes in the media that need to be filled with expert comment and punditry. If you are a second-tier organisation trying to raise your profile by demonstrating your expertise then "expert interviews" could prove an ideal opportunity.

Risk level: low. *If you don't know your stuff you won't be made to look a fool; you simply won't be quoted. You won't be called back next time, however, so make sure you do.*

▼ Promotional

Nice if you can get it. If you can make your new service or product sufficiently exciting and different, the media will see it as being of relevance and interest to their audiences. Just don't expect them to be interested in "me-too" products, or to write about yours just because they wrote about a competitor's. Get a good PR on board who can spot the opportunities, develop your key messages and knows who exactly is likely to be interested.

Risk level: medium. It can be a great opportunity to spread the word and get the brand name out there, but if they don't like what you've done, they can be very blunt.

▼ Responsibility

This is where it gets interesting. It's the occasion when the buck stops with you, and you have to explain what has happened on a matter of public interest, good or bad. Lots of organisations put themselves through crisis media training to be able to cope with media challenges if there is some sort of disaster and they have to be answerable for what has gone wrong. Whether it is hospital trusts or exam boards in the public sector, or food, chemical or transport companies in the private sector, there is scope for catastrophe or at least major embarrassment. Of course, these are worst-case scenarios; much more often it will be a quoted company CEO explaining why the profits of the business are up or down, a fund manager talking about the performance of his or her fund, or the water company representative explaining what steps they are taking to cut leaks.

Many organisations take the opportunity of this kind of interview to get a promotional element in as well. Justin King, for several years boss of the Sainsbury's supermarket chain, has been a good example of this. Whenever interviewed about the company's results on television or radio, he has also included mention of the latest special offers or product success stories. You should not try to push *this too far, however; you can risk it appearing as though you are doing too much of a selling job and are avoiding the actual subject of the interview. Ensure you have had recent, high-quality media training.*

Risk level: high. *There is danger here if there have been any problems for your organisation.*

▼ Beneficiary/Victim

Something beyond your control has taken place and you have been affected; reporters want your reaction. Say your industry sector benefits from a tax change. Reporters may want to know matters such as how much difference it will make to your business, whether will you be investing more, and whether you will be creating more jobs. New regulations are proposed that will increase your costs. How much difference will it make to you? Will it put you out of business? Do you think the government has really thought through the effects of the changes? Or, are you making a lot of fuss over something that is long overdue?

Risk level: low. *So long as you are able to clearly justify your position, and do not appear to be making a lot of fuss about nothing, these types of interview can be a great opportunity to get your name out there and the public on your side.*

▼ Profile/Personality piece

This could be a business feature about your organisation as a success story or one under threat, or a "CEO interview" piece to get your views as a senior figure about what you've been up to recently and your take on where things are going in the sector. These are most typically long-form interviews, an hour or two face-to-face rather than a fifteen-minute phone conversation. They can prove a great opportunity to set the agenda and position yourself as a forward-thinking, authoritative leader in your field.

Risk level: medium. *You need to put much preparation and thought into this kind of interview, as there is time to go into things in some depth, potentially exposing weaknesses or getting on to topics you don't want to discuss, such as future product plans or your views on what the competition is up to. You can also find yourself being asked personal questions about your hobbies and outside interests, and family life. You have to decide whether you are willing to be drawn on such matters. This type of interview can be a great, high-profile opportunity. However, if you do not hit it off with the reporter, you may be painted in an unflattering light in the finished article.*

▼ Celebrity/Notoriety

There can be few people who haven't at one time or another glanced through the celebrity magazines; some people are obsessed by them. Tabloid newspapers also devote pages and pages to people who sometimes just seem to be "famous for being famous". This is the realm of film actresses, reality television show stars and errant footballers. You are unlikely to see yourself in this category, although it is a route some serious business people have taken, wittingly or unwittingly. Sir Richard Branson certainly counts as a celebrity, and what about the panel on the Dragons' Den television show? Their profile has certainly led to more business opportunities coming their way. James Malinchak, a US public speaking coach, appeared on the US version of The Secret Millionaire, aired on the ABC network. Malinchak makes no secret of the fact that he has systematically used this exposure to build his own business, leveraging his fame to create further media opportunities, massively increasing his income.

Risk level: medium. *To get into this category usually requires luck, and for you to be very much the entrepreneurial as opposed to the corporate type, with a clear game plan of what you want to get out of raising your profile to this extent. Remember that what goes up tends to come down; any business or personal problems you hit will become fair game for the media.*

▼ **Technical clarification**

This is a variation on the expert/pundit type of interview. A reporter has to write about the effects of changes in pensions legislation, or a piece on how a new type of electric car battery works. Who are they going to call? They need somebody who actually understands these things, and maybe your organisation has the right kind of expertise. You can use this to build media relationships, and to position yourself as the leading-edge expert in the field.

Risk level: low. *You are doing them a favour by helping them to write the article, so they are usually happy to give you credit. Next time you have something you'd like the media to shout about, you have the right connections in place.*

Rules of engagement – on and off the record

The default setting for how a newspaper or magazine reporter will operate is on this basis: "You know I'm a journalist and you know what publication I represent, and therefore I assume you are happy for anything you say to me to appear in any article I may choose to write." Traditions and practices may vary slightly in different parts of the world, but if nothing else is said, you should operate on this understanding. Some reporters will be very solicitous – "Is it OK if I quote you on this?" Others will say nothing and just assume that because you are happy to talk to them, they can quote you verbatim.

There is a lot of confusion about the phrase "off the record". Once upon a time this may have been material that is purely for background, and not to appear in any article. Now, for most reporters, it means "not for attribution" – in other words, it is understood to mean that the information can appear, but the name of the source shouldn't appear anywhere near it. If you do not want what you say to feature at all, perhaps including it during the interview because you want to give a better understanding of a sensitive issue or steer the reporter away from writing something that is inaccurate, make this 100% clear beforehand, and get their agreement that it is not to appear anywhere in any form. Normally it is in reporters' interests to stick to their word in this area, as they will soon find that no one returns their calls if they get a reputation for being untrustworthy. However, even if they go against their word and publish, they have not broken any law – so you always need to decide whether you are willing to take the risk.

One trick interviewees occasionally get caught by is the "on the way back to the lift" question. This is when a face-to-face interview appears to have concluded, the reporter has closed his or her notebook, and the chief executive (or whoever) politely says, "Let me show you out." Chatting informally while waiting for the lift, the journalist slips in one more question, and the interviewee, now relaxed and thinking the formal proceedings have concluded, chats openly and says more than is wise – perhaps giving the "killer quote" that of course finds its way into a prominent place in the article. Remember, it's not over until it's over.

Some organisations have a rule that they will only allow their spokespeople to talk to journalists on the basis that they will be allowed to see the quotes before they appear in the finished article – otherwise, no deal. This can be appropriate in some circumstances, for example, where financially sensitive material is involved, or the piece covers a technical topic and you are not sure that the reporter has fully understood what you have said – you do not want a mangled quote to appear, perhaps making you look silly in print. My advice is to try not to make this too much of a blanket policy, however – under time pressure, reporters will simply ignore you because of the hassle-factor and go to someone else for comment. If you do want quote approval, try to be friendly about agreeing the rules where possible, rather than laying down the law – you might be able to say something such as, "I'm happy to talk to you, but would it be OK if you could run the quotes by me before they appear? I know there's a lot of confusion surrounding this and I want to be sure I've made it as clear as I can."

While some journalists and publications will not countenance quote approval, others such as trade and technical media may be more relaxed, or even welcome it as a means of ensuring accuracy. It is very helpful for both sides if you correct any misspellings of names, or spot obvious errors such as when they wrote down "billion" although you actually said "million". What you should certainly *not* do is routinely use this process as a means of back-tracking on things you have said. Reporters will want to use your strongest quotes, and if you feel afterwards you have been a little too controversial and start removing them or making them much blander, they will not be at all happy. If there is a good pre-existing relationship, however, your PR may be able to negotiate something.

There is more on the rules of engagement when meeting journalists in informal situations in chapter 6.

Key Reminders

- *If you get to understand how journalists think and operate, you will find it easier to know what they are looking for, to build relationships, and to deliver useful material to them. Understand the importance of deadlines and return a journalist's calls as soon as possible. Get to know deadlines for your key publications if you can.*

- *Reporters will seek different points of view on a story; if they fail to reflect yours, that doesn't always mean they've got it wrong. You will have to accept the rough with the smooth.*

- *They are highly unlikely to be as knowledgeable as you about your subject; try to communicate in jargon-free plain language, and do not assume knowledge. Offer help on technical subjects.*

- *Do not try to be too clever and "spin" your story to journalists – stick to the truth. Resist any temptation to exaggerate or lie; if you lose their trust, it is probably gone forever.*

- *A surprising percentage of the stories carried in magazines, newspapers and broadcasting are PR-generated, creating a lot of opportunities. If you don't grab them, someone else will.*

- *There are different types of media interviews, and you are likely to be treated rather differently if you are being interviewed as a pundit or "expert" than if you are being asked to take responsibility for a problem involving your* company. Make sure you are clear beforehand about what sort of role you are expected to fulfil, and which of the seven main interview types you should expect.

- Understand the rules of engagement with journalists – "off the record" does not necessarily or even typically mean that something cannot appear in the article, just that it should be "unattributable". You cannot usually expect to be able to check quotes before they appear.

Chapter 3

Seven big mistakes companies make when dealing with the media

Keep your priorities balanced

FACTOR

Seven big mistakes companies make when dealing with the media

Those organisations and individuals with the M-factor have learned, usually by trial and error, to avoid these common mistakes.

ONE: slow speed of response

Some years ago when working on business programmes for BBC Radio, I can vividly remember calling up a leading City law firm late one afternoon, trying to find an expert to explain the effects of a big change in European competition law on UK takeovers for our listeners that evening. The response? "Oh, I'm afraid the person who deals with that sort of thing has gone home. Could you call again on Monday?" As you can imagine, we were highly unlikely to come back to these people for comment in a hurry. It was a great opportunity missed to position themselves as the experts on a key issue for big British companies. Instead, we gave the airtime to their biggest competitors.

Admittedly, this was some time ago, and the media handling skills of professional services firms have (on the whole) sharpened up a lot since then. But slow speed of response is still a common failing. Usually the media relations team is all too aware of the reporter's time constraints, but CEOs and senior managers are busy people and have too many other things on their plates. It is smart to prioritise any serious media enquiry where possible, not to leave it as number seven on the 'to do' list. When journalists need comment, they often put calls out to at least a couple of rival firms – the early bird usually catches the headline.

For instance, on news of a proposed tax change, correspondents covering the story for national newspapers will probably put calls out to two or three of the large accountancy firms. They don't always know who will respond quickly, and who will have something interesting to say, so they prefer to cover themselves – otherwise there is a risk they will hit their deadline with no material. Similarly if there are new proposals on food labelling, they won't just call one supermarket. Try to ensure that your organisation is usually able to respond with a couple of strong points to make within half an hour or so if this is a relevant issue for you, involving influential publications or broadcast outlets. Remember, unless you already have more media attention than you can handle, you are aiming to raise your profile as an authoritative voice. Of course it is sensible to prioritise – many large companies get far more media requests than they can deal with, and it is not always worthwhile or possible to drop everything, but always do what you can to help your key target publications and channels – you may be the one desperate for their help next time.

Even if you are 'within deadline' it may effectively be too late. For instance, suppose a reporter calls up the media relations department at 10.30am saying that they need something by 12.30pm at the latest. You are busy with meetings but manage to return the call at 12.20pm. The reporter may be finishing off his or her piece and may well say, "Thanks, but I've got all I need now from someone else." Even if they are still keen to speak, you are much less likely to be able to set the agenda, compared to your rival who called him back at 11am. Nearly all publications now have websites, and there is pressure on many journalists to get stories up online as soon as possible. This has tended to conflate the whole process even further over recent years. Sometimes, regrettably, speed can triumph over accuracy.

If there is a big announcement, the radio and television news channels will aim for informed response live on air within a few minutes. This is daunting for most people, but a chance for those who are keen to raise their profile to grab the opportunity to 'have a view'. The channel concerned will often be so grateful that you've been willing to help out that they will be eating out of your hand in the future. This does not mean that you have to overdo it, pushing yourself forward anywhere and everywhere, only that you should try to take the right opportunity when it is offered, as the chance may not come up again.

At the other end of the time-scale, even the Sunday papers no longer have 'all week' to write their stories, as a lot of people imagine. Many are part of seven-day operations with their daily counterparts, and the majority of their stories are written in the latter part of the week. The various sections and supplements, such as property, personal finance and motoring, will often have deadlines much earlier in the week so that sub-editors and printing capacity can be freed up for the time-sensitive stuff as publication day approaches. Very often the reporter will be lucky to have more than half a day to work on a story. So again the speed of response really matters.

Reporters are not completely unreasonable people – otherwise they would never get anyone to talk to them. They do not expect every conversation to be open-ended. If you are in a rush, it is better to call back quickly and say, "Look I'm really sorry but I can only give you ten minutes because I have to go into a meeting at 3pm," than leave it until you come out of the meeting at 4pm, by which time it may be too late. Of course, spokespeople should always follow the rule of finding out exactly what the reporter is looking for, to give themselves time to prepare a couple of good points to make, before having a substantive conversation with them – more on this in chapter 5.

TWO: not understanding what the market wants

It's like the old British industry problem of 'trying to sell what we can make' rather than 'trying to make what the market wants to buy'. In my time as a business journalist I spoke to many people who wondered why reporters weren't very interested in their new product (which was much like everybody else's new product) or their 'authoritative industry survey' on the effects of new European Union regulations on smaller Italian insurance companies, or tedious equivalent. Only the most specialist of trade publications can really get excited about this sort of thing, and they can be a very hard sell to the nationals. The business and City desks are used to the thud of dreary-looking 'surveys' from big consultancy firms falling upon them, or pinging into their in-boxes, each with an optimistic press release attached, attempting to make it look newsworthy.

Often people are simply too self-promotional – focused only on what is of interest to *them,* not to the reader, viewer or listener. Try instead to put yourself in the audience's shoes. Spend a bit of time actually watching the shows and reading the publications you are most likely to deal with, to see what appears to float their boat.

The most media-savvy organisations focus on what their target publications are writing about, and look to see if they can deliver pithy and relevant comment on the hot issues. As one prominent Sunday newspaper Business Editor put it, *"I am too often pitched ideas that do not take the story forward, but only comment on things that have already happened."* (He sees that as the role of the dailies.) The television news channels and radio shows are looking for people with strong opinions, not those who are meticulously and boringly even-handed. This is a challenge and means that not every opportunity is an appropriate one – but do think through how you might be able to use each one positively, before rejecting it out of hand.

Smart firms aim to use the media to position themselves as 'thought leaders' – although this is not a phrase to be used in front of journalists, who tend to be pretty dismissive of such corporate-speak. Logically, therefore, the idea is to find out what publications clients and prospective clients tend to read – and try to build relationships with the editors of those publications. Don't get obsessed by the trade magazines if they are mostly seen by your competitors rather than customers.

THREE: thinking you can wing it

Once you are clear about your priority points as a spokesperson, rehearse them to ensure that they will come across as strongly as possible. Otherwise, they will not be front of mind when you speak to the journalist, or for that matter customers, clients or other stakeholders. The clearer you are about your interview objectives in this area, the more your subconscious will be looking for ways to bring these points to the fore; see chapter 5 for more on formulating these. Particularly if you have a broadcast interview coming up, there is no substitute for having practice in saying what you want to say out loud. It is only then that you will realise whether the points will be jargon-free, will flow and be convincing.

Do not be afraid of a certain amount of repetition in the interview; repeat points where appropriate, but try to find different ways of framing them each time. Phrases such as 'As I was saying' and 'As I've already explained' can legitimise this. Otherwise, the danger is that the things you really want the interviewer or audience to remember will be lost among all the other stuff. You want, if possible, the point you most want to be picked up to be the most compelling one you make, so it stands out as the obvious quote to be used. Running it through a few times beforehand will make a big difference. Don't think you can just wing it – that is when mistakes get made.

FOUR: not having enough 'oven-ready' spokespeople

You could argue that this particularly applies to radio and television shows, which at a national level cannot afford to have nervous, incoherent spokespeople who will make the channel as well as themselves look bad. The frequent appearance of the same old cast of regulars is because the producer knows they will deliver, and does not want to get it in the neck by putting forward an untried name who then goes on and does not perform. You need to be confident that when you put somebody forward to represent your organisation that person can perform, and can perform consistently – after all, they are representing your brand. The ability to use clear, jargon-free language is important here (see chapter 4).

Key spokespeople should be smart enough to keep their media skills in trim by having 'refresher' media training every so often, and by taking opportunities to appear on smaller radio stations or to talk to journalists from more obscure publications – it's all good practice for when the big invitation comes to appear on *Newsnight*, or for when the nationals are showing interest. When that opportunity comes up, it is nearly always too late to arrange the training – there is unlikely to be time for much more than a quick bit of interview practice with your PR adviser. Even managers who might occasionally speak to trade journalists but are unlikely to ever appear on television can benefit massively from appropriate coaching – otherwise they are likely to miss opportunities to get their points across, and are much more likely to find themselves being misquoted or saying something they hadn't planned to say. Poor media training can be counterproductive, however, if it turns people into 'corporate robots', parroting their lines and avoiding the questions – get it done properly.

Do not rely on just one spokesperson; he or she may be on holiday, or ill, or otherwise unavailable. It is especially important to train up the next generation who can step in when required – this can demonstrate to the media that there is strength in depth at your organisation. You do not want the media to get the impression that it is a one-man show. I can think of more than one business which had benefited for years from a high media profile, leading to a steady stream of clients and referrals, but which had vested only one individual with the role of handling all the interviews. The person selected may have become a very practised and lively speaker, much in demand, but when he or she left their respective company the media profile of the organisation vanished with them.

FIVE: not getting to the point

Far too many subject experts just waffle on when talking to reporters, rarely getting to the point. Journalists have time constraints and if they fail to understand what you are going on about then they are likely to quickly make their excuses and move on to the next person. Lawyers and academics tend to marshal the evidence, put the case on either side, and then reach a conclusion – but this is not the approach to follow. It sounds pretty logical, but journalists tend to construct their stories the opposite way around – headline first, followed by a first paragraph summarising the key findings, followed by evidence and detail only so far as space allows. This is the approach you should follow in an interview. Too often the reporter asks the 'expert' a question and then has to listen for what seems like several minutes before they get to the nub of the issue – by which time they may have lost interest.

Ensure spokespeople prepare properly, and are ready with their key points and conclusions so that even if the reporter is short of time, he or she won't lose sight of the important bits. Some spokespeople do need quite a lot of practice at this! Of course this is especially pertinent for those appearing on radio or television – if an answer appears to be meandering, interviewers tend to interrupt and move the discussion on. It is particularly important to be clear before you pick up the phone to speak to the journalist that you know the specific points you want to convey.

For these reasons, if a reporter rings you up directly then you should always create some thinking time before giving your comments. Ask the reporter what they are looking for, where you fit into the story and when they need your input by – these are the sorts of questions your media relations experts would normally ask if they take the call. Then tell them you are right in the middle of something or are about to go into a meeting, but that you will call them back as soon as you have finished – always get a direct line number. Use the time to work out the key points you want to get across – then you can have a focused, waffle-free conversation when you are ready, but not before.

By the way, you can create this thinking time even if you are face-to-face with a journalist, for example at an industry conference. You have just given a presentation, and a reporter comes up to you wanting further comment. If you are ready to deal with these questions, fine – otherwise, there is no need to feel cornered. If you are not the relevant person to deal with the issue, suggest they call your media relations team. If the buck stops with you, say you will be very happy to chat briefly before you have to be on your way, but you have a couple of urgent calls to make before you do anything else. Go off and call up your media relations person to clarify what points you should be getting across. Then you can have a focused conversation saying what you want to say, rather than an unhelpful, defensive, round-the-houses conversation.

SIX: slavishly following the reporter's agenda

Inexperienced interviewees are usually a little nervous beforehand, particularly in the case of a television or radio interview. Their objective is primarily to survive the interview, without making fools of themselves or saying something dreadful. They try to answer each question as best they can, but perhaps without stopping to think about whether what they are saying is useful or relevant, either to themselves or to the viewers or listeners. They may get to the end of the interview just to realise that they have not said what they wanted to say at all. This is rather more common than you might realise, and happens also with print journalists, who can take you off in all sorts of directions you had not expected – more on dealing with this in chapter 5.

The key is to remember that it is *your* interview – after all, they have asked to speak to *you*, and are seeking *your* views. So if you think a particular point is important, then it probably is important. Of course, this is not a licence to be like the politician who never answers the question – the opposite of M-factor behaviour. This is about an exchange where there is something in it for both sides. You should do your best to answer the questions they have for you, but at the same time you have the chance to make the points you wish to make – so long as they are relevant.

SEVEN: giving away more than you should

While journalists get very frustrated by the people who hardly say anything in interviews, they rub their hands with glee thinking of the many others who say far too much – the 'loose cannons'. Often these people are too polite – if asked a question, they feel obliged to answer it, whether they really want to or not. Remember, it is the reporter's job to ask whatever questions he or she thinks appropriate – there is no necessity, however, for you to answer all of them, or to do so in great detail. Sometimes they are just trying it on, in the hope of a lucky break.

The problem here is that you can reveal far more to the market, including your competitors, than you want to. I have seen people, under the gentlest of prodding, talk about future product plans in far more detail than they should, and give off-the-cuff views that are far from thought through. Remember that if you casually mention to a trade reporter that you are looking at launching 'product X' in the third quarter of the year, that might make for far more of a story than the points you wanted to get across in the interview. So, what happens is this. Your message gets lost, the headline is instead all about plans for Product X, and your marketing and PR people are tearing their hair out because their carefully-laid plans to announce Product X in a couple of months' time have now had all element of surprise removed. The journalists will not want to write about X at the appropriate time because by then it will be old news. You have also given your competitors notice of your plans, making it easier for them to bring forward anything similar they have in the pipeline and beat you to it.

On anything contentious, you need to be clear beforehand about your boundaries. Do not lie about your plans (ever) but if necessary you can say something generic such as, "We are looking at various options in that area but haven't made any final decisions." (There are more suggestions for ways to hold the line in chapter 7.) Sometimes reporters will try to get you to give your views on what your rivals are up to; the rule in most companies is that you should avoid directly criticising competitor products and activities (there are exceptions, such as airlines Ryanair and Virgin Atlantic). It is better to focus on the strengths of what you are doing – otherwise your comments may be positioned in the finished article as an out-and-out attack on the other company. There is nothing the press likes more than a spat between two competing organisations.

Another technique reporters will sometimes use is just to let you carry on talking, in the hope you will find yourself filling the silence to keep the conversation going – adding just that bit extra that you should have kept to yourself. If you have said all you want to say on a topic, just stop – the reporter is probably a bit behind you anyway, trying to jot down the points you have been making. It is then up to them to come up with another question; you have also given yourself a bit of thinking time. Alternatively, this is a great opportunity to move on to one of your key messages, or your Extras – see chapter 5 for techniques on how to do this.

Key Reminders

The seven big mistakes people make when dealing with the media:

1 *Slow speed of response. Journalists usually work to tight time-frames – you are more likely to build relationships and get good coverage if you respond quickly to their requests. If you are seeking to raise your profile, you need them more than they need you.*

2 *Not understanding what the market wants. You will usually get further by finding out what they are interested in and then trying to deliver it, than by trying to persuade them to be interested in what you find fascinating.*

3 *Not practising/rehearsing. Once you have identified your key points, say them out loud to help you find the most powerful and effective ways of putting them across.*

4 *Not having enough 'oven-ready' spokespeople. Have a cadre of well media-trained individuals who can step up where necessary, otherwise you will miss opportunities or flounder when there are tough issues.*

5 *Not getting to the point. Too many subject experts waffle or get bogged down in detail, because they are unable to see the wood from the trees. Prioritise the key points; the rest can come later. Always give yourself time to prepare these points before you speak to a reporter.*

6 *Slavishly following the questions. Try to give reporters everything they need, but lead the conversation if necessary to cover the points you feel are most important.*

7 *Saying too much. You do not have to answer every question if the material is confidential or commercially sensitive. Be clear where your boundaries lie.*

Chapter 4

The art of the soundbite: making your interview memorable

Aim to be memorable, but not too memorable

FACTOR

The art of the soundbite: making your interview memorable

When you say it, say it well. Ask any print or broadcast journalist, and they will tell you that there are M-factor people who just 'get it' and who are a delight to interview, while with others it is like drawing blood from a stone. So what differentiates the two types? Having a lively and engaging style comes naturally to some people; others have to work at it. When dealing with the media it is vital to give yourself a little time to prepare, so you can maximise your chances of sparkling.

First, the reporter wants you to be able to come up with some good content, as we will see in the next chapter. The second thing he or she is looking for is a good 'quote' – usually known by television and radio reporters as a 'soundbite'. The great thing here is that even if the point you want to get across in your interview is not very earth-shattering or original – and practically anyone in your industry could have made it, if you say it in a sharper, punchier way than the competition, you are still being more useful to the journalist than they are. It is about adding value. Do this consistently and the publication or channel will come back to you time and again, meaning that it will be your organisation setting the agenda, not someone else's.

The term 'soundbite' was first used in the 1970s, and is defined as a short, memorable statement, as used by politicians, often designed to be picked up by a television news bulletin. Originally interview clips used on the news were often about thirty seconds in length, but they are usually a lot shorter in the UK now and shorter still (less than ten seconds) in the US. The core soundbite phrase is typically only a sentence or two long. One of the most famous, because of its self-referential nature, came from Tony Blair as prime minister in 1998, in the run-up to the Good Friday agreement being reached in Northern Ireland.

"A day like today is not a day for soundbites, really.
But I feel the hand of history upon our shoulders, I really do."

Memorable, but he did lay himself open to ridicule, as having said it wasn't a day for soundbites, this was clearly a prime example. On this occasion it may possibly have been something Blair just happened to say in response to a reporter's question, but more frequently the best, most memorable phrases have been carefully crafted beforehand. Don't think that, unlike the professionals, you will simply be able to come up with your best material on the spot.

Some memorable soundbites

"Ask not what your country can do for you
– ask what you can do for your country."

— President John F. Kennedy, inaugural address, 1961

"My Administration is the only thing between
you and the pitchforks."

— President Barack Obama, reflecting public anger at the bankers,
when he called a group of Wall Street CEOs to Washington, 2009

"We have fourteen days to save the NHS
[National Health Service]."

— Prime Minister Tony Blair, election campaign, 1997

"Derivatives are financial weapons of mass destruction."

—Warren Buffett, legendary investor

"I'm the only person I know that's lost a quarter of a billion dollars in one year.... It's very character-building."

—Steve Jobs, quoted in the book Apple Confidential 2.0, on the company's near-demise in the 1990s

The 'EQuALS' formula

It would be lovely for journalists if every interview included a memorable phrase like one of these, but of course that is not going to happen. Fortunately, there are plenty of other ways you can get yourself quoted by going beyond the generic and the dull. Use the EQuALS formula to ensure you are 'adding value' by coming up with at least one of these. If you want to be cheesy about it, remember 'preparation EQuALS success'.

E	stands for	EXAMPLES
Qu	stands for	QuOTES
A	stands for	ANECDOTES
L	stands for	LIKENESSES
S	stands for	STATISTICS

Examples

You need to flesh out your key points with verbal and visual aids – anything that helps to illustrate the point you are trying to make and relates it to real life for readers, viewers or listeners. Once you have made your point, use a phrase such as 'so for instance' to lead you seamlessly into something more specific. So, when British Airways introduced beds in first class on its transatlantic routes in the late 1990s it didn't just say that passengers would be able to sleep more easily in-flight. Its press releases added a lot more descriptive, specific detail, bringing the experience alive in the reader's imagination; this example was aimed at the US market, hence the spelling: "The first class cabin will have fourteen individual modules, giving each customer more private space and comfort. They will have the opportunity to sleep the air miles away in a completely flat six-foot, six-inch bed under a cozy duvet with full size pillows, plus special pajamas."

Quotes

I am thinking here of the more memorable, crafted quotes or soundbites mentioned earlier. You probably do not have the time to sit down and come up with one of these – after all, people like Tony Blair and Warren Buffett had scriptwriters and advisers to help with theirs. Sometimes a little brainstorming with colleagues and your PR team can work magic; at other times you will pick up a phrase that stands out from a colleague or client at a meeting. Don't be afraid to plagiarise. If it worked for them, it can probably work for you – after all, they probably heard it themselves first from somebody else. If you are still stumped, don't worry – use something else from the EQuALS formula.

Anecdotes

People relate to stories, not dry, generic points. For example, reporters always want eyewitness accounts of a disaster, as they are much more memorable. People can see they are genuine, not second- or third-hand reports that have been through some sort of editorial filter. They will make your message much more quotable. Don't tell us that your customers like a particular product feature, tell us about someone in particular you were talking to, and how in specific terms they benefited. Try to put yourself in readers' or viewers' shoes. Rather than saying, "The economy is developing very fast in Brazil," a point anyone could make, perhaps you could say,

"The pace of change in Brazil is extraordinarily rapid at the moment – I've just come back from a trip to São Paulo, and there's a massive difference compared to my last visit ten years ago, you should see..." and then go on to paint a picture of what you witnessed with your own eyes. Personal stories like this are more quotable, and they boost your credibility as someone who really does know what they are talking about, as opposed to someone who just sits behind their desk all day and pretends to know.

Likenesses

Simile, metaphor, comparisons for the purpose of emphasising a point (it was a 'drop in the ocean') – these can all make your message more powerful, or clearer to somebody by enabling them to visualise something that might otherwise be unfamiliar. Here are some examples of similes and metaphors that are much more effective than simply saying someone looked a mess, or had been through a hard time, or was looking at something nearly 90 feet tall.

"He looked as if he'd been dragged through a hedge backwards."

"It was a nightmare."

"It was the height of six London double-decker buses."

Or, suppose you are part of a campaign group wanting to get the water company to fix a number of small leaks in its pipes. If you complain that put together they are leaking 2,500 cubic metres of water every day, that may sound a lot but it equally is impossible to visualise for a lot of people. If you say it is the equivalent of an Olympic-size swimming pool every day, that means much more. Just be careful you do not draw an analogy or use a metaphor that means one thing to you, but might be meaningless or have an entirely different meaning to other people, who may have different frames of reference. If you make the point that you offer a 'Rolls-Royce service' that might imply to you that your service is of high quality; to someone else it might imply 'very expensive'. Try out any fancy phrases or metaphors on a colleague or two first, to ensure they do the right job for you.

Statistics

A telling fact can really clinch the argument and convince a reporter or television audience. If you tell me, "Lots of people use their smartphones for food shopping," I may or may not believe you. If you say, "In 2011 Deloitte carried out research which showed that more than 40% of American smartphone owners used it for food shopping, and I suspect the figure is quite a lot higher now," it sounds like you know what you are talking about. Always be on the lookout for the 'killer fact' that can back up your main arguments. However, a word of warning: one or two powerful statistics can be enormously useful, and they will make it much more likely that these key points will be used in the article or report, as they clearly have evidence to back them up, but too many statistics soon gets confusing. The more facts and figures you throw at a reporter, the more likely the reporter is to get something wrong through failing to keep up with you. You may think you are being helpful by filling in lots of background, but in fact you are probably being the opposite. Ensure that your most powerful evidence is backing up the points you want to see reported, rather than distracting attention from them. By the way, *S* could also stand for *Superlatives* – journalists always keep an ear open for words like 'biggest' and 'fastest', which can turn an otherwise mundane fact into more of a story.

Avoid the jargon trap

Every industry has its jargon; think of those TLAs (three-letter-acronyms) or even FLAs (five-letter-acronyms) in your own sector. The financial sector, the military/defence sector, the tech sector, the pharmaceutical sector, you name it – they are all as bad as each other when it comes to having a catalogue of technical terms, which are a mystery to those outside. On top of this, many organisations have their own shorthand, built up over years, for use within the business. Of course what this means is that you may be one of those people who spend 95% of their working lives speaking in this impenetrable language, which means you have to work that much harder every time you have to translate for someone external. Some people do not even bother, imagining, mysteriously, that the journalist will know just as much about their industry as they do, and be aware of all the current terminology.

Some will, of course – the specialist correspondents who have been around for a long time, and maybe those who came from the industry themselves, and moved into journalism. The rest may be struggling. Many reporters (for instance, in the business sections of the nationals) have to cover a wide range of topics. On other occasions, the specialist is away covering something else, and another person has to fill in, doing the best they can. The trade publications usually have a blend of youth and experience. You may find yourself talking to a bright 22 year-old who was on a postgraduate journalism course not long ago, and is now on a steep learning curve trying to get the hang of your sector. You are part of his or her educational process. Other times you will speak to an experienced reporter but one who has just moved beat – the *Financial Times* (*FT*) is one of those publications which deliberately moves its specialists around, so that they do not 'go native', and will continue to come at things from a fresh rather than a jaded perspective.

In fact, I think this is one of the biggest single reasons that people get misquoted in the papers: it is because the journalist has not quite understood what a contact has said, and they do not like to seek clarification for fear of how it will make them look. Particularly the younger, less experienced journalists will not always be comfortable admitting that they do not know things, hoping that it will 'all become clear' in the end. So the lesson is: use the everyday option whenever you can. If use of jargon or technical language is essential, spell them out in full when you first introduce them, so the reporter can easily keep up and does not lose the meaning. For instance, rather than saying, "Obviously falling ARPU is a big issue for the industry at the moment," you might instead say, "As you know, the industry is very concerned about falling Average Revenue Per User at the moment, or ARPU..." The explanation has only taken a few extra seconds but has ensured that the reporter hasn't misunderstood you and maybe even missed your next point, because they are struggling to work out what you have just said.

Some people say, "Imagine you are explaining it to an intelligent twelve year-old." I think there is a danger of talking down to the reporter if you do that, so I would say, "Imagine someone has asked you a question at a family party" – in that situation you are forced to be clear, and would not get far if you tried to be pompous or patronising. Of course, lots of people do not even realise they are speaking in jargon, as it all feels so everyday and normal to them. If so, apply the 'pub test'. That is, imagine you went along with a clipboard and asked 100 patrons of your nearest public house what various industry terms meant. Realistically, what percentage do you think would know the answer? If the answer is a fairly low proportion, you know you need to explain as you go – certainly for a radio or television audience, and probably to a newspaper or magazine reporter if you think he or she is not a specialist in your area.

It is better practice, and more quotable, to speak in plain English anyway. Here are some examples of corporate-speak you could profitably dispense with, if you haven't already.

Jargon and business-speak

Avoid if possible	Better instead
"End-users"	"People"/"Customers"
"Granular level"	"In more detail"
"Going forward"	"From now on"/ "Looking ahead"
"Looking at the consumer space"	"So far as the consumer market's concerned"
"Paradigm shift"	"Big change"
"We don't have the bandwidth"	"We don't have the capacity"
"Pushing the envelope"	"Taking it as far as we can"
"Thinking outside the box"	"Thinking creatively"
"Our channel strategy"	"Our distribution plans"
"We offer world-class solutions"	"We believe we're among the best"
"Customer/Value proposition"	"What we offer"/"What makes us different"
"We have a results-driven mindset"	"We really focus on getting results"
"It's a value-added deliverable"	"It gives customers extra/ something they really value"
"It's a scalable solution"	"It's easy to expand"

... and so on. Ask your colleagues/family which bits of jargon annoy them .

Additional techniques

What else could make your interview more successful, and efficient as a way of transmitting information to a publication, radio or television show and its audience? Here are some tips and techniques which the more experienced interviewee will use, often without anyone noticing what they are up to.

Repeat

A degree of repetition is no bad thing, and is particularly important for driving the key points home. Remember, if you chat to a print journalist for twenty minutes, he or she is unlikely to use more than a couple of sentences of what you have said in the average article. So if you say twenty things, eighteeen of them are likely to be left out. You have no idea of what will make the cut. By contrast, if you return to your main point two or three times during the interview, it is very clear to the reporter that this is what you believe is important. You can help by using expressions such as, "But as I was saying" or "But coming back to my earlier point". Or, you could use the technique popular when making presentations – "Tell 'em what you're going to tell 'em, tell 'em, and then tell 'em what you've told 'em." This has to be more subtle in an interview context, but the principle of setting up your ideas at the beginning, and then going into more detail, and then reiterating the main points by way of conclusion at the end, can still be very effective. So when a journalist asks their first question, rather than going straight in you can preface your answer by saying something like, "Well I think there are two areas of concern here, the principle of what's being proposed, and the sheer red tape angle." You have already placed firmly in the reporter's mind the idea that they should be conveying both these aspects in the finished piece.

Flag

This is a related technique to the above, aimed again at improving the chance of the reporter picking up what you want them to pick up, not getting sidetracked with something that may catch their attention but which you believe to be peripheral. You simply flag, as clearly as you can, the bits that you feel really matter, so it is absolutely clear to the journalist what you believe should appear in the piece if your views are to be fairly reflected. Of course, the finished article is up to the reporter – you cannot tell them what to write, and if you do you will get short shrift. The onus is on you to make your key points as compelling and as relevant as possible, so he or she can instantly see the importance of what you are highlighting. The relevant flagging phrases include "the key point here is", "and this is absolutely at the heart of the matter", "but what is really important" and "though as I was saying, it all comes down to".

Get emotive language on your side

This is something that protest groups, NGOs (non-governmental organisations), trade unions and so on are usually brilliant at, but big corporates are usually hopeless with, perhaps because they are used to all that dreary corporate-speak. If you use emotive phrases in your interview like, "It would be a disaster if..." or "This will have dire consequences," they are much more powerful and headline-worthy than "We are worried about..." or "This is likely to have a negative effect on..." If you want your quotes to be lost somewhere down in the middle of the piece, or to not feature at all, use dull language. If you want to stand out and set the agenda, use words that will leave an impression. Here, however, it is even more essential to choose your words carefully in advance. If you are always reactive, you make it easier to let the reporter put words in your mouth. If the interviewer says, "But if that happened, it would be a disaster for you, wouldn't it?" you may find yourself responding, "Well, I wouldn't say it would be a disaster for us, but it would certainly have an impact." You will have then allowed the reporter to frame the story in terms of just how much of a disaster this is going to be for your organisation. The quote will probably read, " 'I wouldn't say it would be a disaster for us, but it would certainly have an impact,' said chief executive Joe Blow..." Readers will assume that it will indeed be a disaster, but you are just trying to put a good face on it. Your interview has effectively been hijacked –with a real danger that the points you wanted to make have been lost, to never make it into the finished article. Better to have used your own words rather than the reporter's – such as, "I believe the impact would be limited, because…"

Key Reminders

■ *You can still be quoted even if what you are saying is not a particularly original point – you just have to say it better. It is worth spending a little time trying to come up with a punchy 'quote' or soundbite.*

■ *Use the EQuALS formula to try to add value to the article or report. Providing examples, 'quotable quotes', anecdotes, likenesses or statistics can all pep up the points you want to make, and increase your hit-rate with the media.*

■ *Jargon is the bane of journalists' lives. Avoid it. If the reporter does not fully understand what you are saying, your views are less likely to be accurately reflected.*

■ *Do not be afraid to repeat your key points in the course of the conversation, so the reporter can easily see what you think is important. Flag up anything you believe to be particularly significant.*

■ *Emotive language is powerful and tends to find its way into the headlines. If you want to set the agenda, use words that have impact.*

■ *Do not let reporters put words into your mouth unless you are happy for them to do so.*

Chapter 5

Defining your key messages

Try to keep your key messages consistent

FACTOR

Defining your key messages

Before you start taking media calls, spend some time with your media relations advisers or your senior team, clarifying the key messages you should be getting across. Some may be what I call 'core messages' about your company, its strengths and positioning, which you should ideally get into almost any interview, while others will be the strongest points you want to make on the specific story of the day – your particular *angle*. If your core messages make it into the finished article or broadcast interview, this can feel akin to achieving some free advertising. A real win. Even if they do not, you are helping the reporter, who is now more likely to describe your business accurately and from a position of knowledge and understanding. He or she will also be more aware of other occasions when you may have something to contribute that they may not otherwise have thought of.

Core and key messages

Your core messages are likely to be very consistent – you do not have to start from scratch every time you speak to a different reporter on a different topic (although you should update the points when relevant). Once you are clear about them, and where possible have also identified some subsidiary matters or 'extras' that you have lined up ready to bring out if appropriate, you can then come up with some relevant things you want to say that will be your angle on the journalist's specific agenda. Together they make up your 'key messages'. Make these positive, unless you are certain you want to go on the attack – a critical remark, perhaps about another company's activities, can become the story, detracting from what you actually wanted to get across. Your aim should be to give reporters something useful, interesting and appropriate every time, so that they go away happy, and therefore likely to write about you in the most constructive way. After all, the question reporters most frequently ask themselves when listening to your answers is, "Yes, but why should my readers care?" That is what you should be addressing.

Your core messages and the specific angle you want to communicate on the topic should be at the heart of the interview, where feasible and relevant. This may sound obvious, but surprising numbers of people who speak to reporters find themselves in purely 'reactive mode', wondering only what the next question will be and hoping they will be able to find an answer. If you can, lead the agenda and take the interview where you want it to go, rather than merely hoping the interviewer has exactly the same agenda as you. This of course does *not* mean you should be like the politicians who seem to ignore the questions entirely, only saying what they want to say, or like a 'corporate robot', who just keeps repeating the company's key messages. You should deal with all relevant and legitimate questions, but equally you shouldn't be afraid to give the conversation a bit of direction. Rather than taking the attitude, "They're the ones asking the questions, it's my job to try to come up with the answers," you should take the view, "It's *my* interview – if they weren't interested in my take on things, they wouldn't have called me up. What do *I* think is important?"

This applies to almost all interviews, except 'responsibility' interviews (see chapter 2); with these, you may be answerable to the public, or to shareholders, or other stakeholders, for your actions. Then, they are the ones who can set the agenda, and it is right and legitimate for the reporter to put questions to you on their behalf, even if those questions are uncomfortable for you to answer. In these circumstances you should still of course try to get across your key points, but you need to be doubly prepared; take the advice of your media relations advisers or PR consultancy, who may have a much better idea of the likely journalistic angles and approaches than you do. There is more on dealing with difficult questions and crises in chapter 7.

Defining your core messages

First, though, you need to have your core messages ready and waiting. So, think about what, in a perfect world, you would like a journalist to write or broadcast about you. Would you like him or her to write that you have a smart, innovative product or service, which is the first of its type to offer a particular feature? If so, ensure you make this point very clearly in your interview; otherwise, they will probably not include it. Certainly this is not something they will hear from your competitors. These messages will usually be self-serving, but the trick is to make them of sufficient interest and relevance – otherwise you will be whistling in the wind. Consider delivering a thirty-second pitch statement that covers what your business does, and where it adds value, and if possible how it differentiates itself. That might be the same for any reporter you speak to, serving to familiarise him or her with your organisation, giving them key facts they may have been unaware of, and demonstrating if you can why you are a "good thing".

If you think a reporter will unquestioningly transcribe me-too material that best belongs in your corporate brochure, you are likely to be disappointed. However, something that credentialises you (for example, industry awards won, impressive turnover figures or rate of customer growth) may well be relevant points to be reported, as they help justify to the reader why the reporter has gone to you for comment rather than anybody else. There is plenty of scope for lots of other interesting, relevant material for the reporter, but you do not want to miss the opportunity to get over what matters to *you*.

While you might aim to end up with a couple of core messages that you would hope to get in to any interview, there may be some others that might be relevant only in particular circumstances. For example, you might be in the toiletries business, and want the world to know you have just made a fascinating deal with a Brazilian partner to open up the Latin American market. However, it is likely to be a waste of time trying to get this across to a consumer reporter, or a trade journalist writing about a technical development in your sector in the UK. If you are talking to a German-based publication about your operations in Europe, it would not be smart only to give UK examples – you would focus more on the relevant market. Similarly, a company providing trading systems to the financial sector may have some key selling points about their ease of use for certain types of traders in investment banks or hedge funds. Save these for the appropriate specialist magazines and ensure you put them across strongly, but do not bore *The Times* or *FT* with such matters, unless they ask, or that is the particular focus of the interview. You want to be able to demonstrate to the reporter that you have thought about what is useful for their particular audience, rather than just hitting them with some irrelevant material that suggests you haven't a clue. So, have a few messages for different markets up your sleeve where possible, ready to be pulled out at the right moment. Remember that your own core or key messages are not the same thing as a story, as some people seem to imagine. The first may be of major interest to you but only of passing interest to the journalist; by contrast, with the second, the opposite can apply.

Your media strategy should be driven by your business objectives, so ensure they are aligned. There is no point in letting the conversation be dominated by a part of the market that is no longer a priority for you, if you can avoid it. You want your strongest points to endorse your positioning in your most promising product areas, so that these are more likely to be picked up by the journalist. Equally you should make sure your PR messages do not in any way appear to be at odds with what your marketing department is saying or doing; there are certainly cases where this has happened, and it does not create the best of impressions.

Ten questions to help you define your organisation's core messages

1 How would we like the outside world to describe us?

2 What do we think makes us different from other similar companies?

3 What is notable about our customer offer or customer service?

4 What have we done that people are most likely to remember us for?

5 What have we done that is pioneering?

6 Where are we market-leading?

7 Are we taking a bet on any big industry trends?

8 What is our most successful product or service?

9 Are there any big issues affecting our market at the moment (eg regulatory change) where we would like to make our voice heard?

10 Is there anything about our company style or culture that makes us stand out?

Jot down what genuine points you could make on any of these which are relevant. Pick out the strongest of these points; the list should provide an indicator of where your priorities should be focused. The great thing about these messages is that once you are clear about them in your own mind, you do not have to keep reinventing them. The core points about your business, its strengths, the benefits of its products and what differentiates you from competitors, gradually evolve but rarely change overnight. Therefore, you can put them across in any or every interview. You can define them either at company level, or if appropriate at divisional or product level. Do not worry about some repetition – if you cannot get across a consistent message about your business, how can you expect the public, or your customers, to have a clear idea of what you are all about? The interview is your opportunity to reinforce these messages if you can.

Consistency with others in your organisation is also of course highly important – everyone in your business area who is media-facing should be endorsing the same core points where possible. I am often surprised when working with organisations of all types to find that they are remarkably vague on what they are trying to convey. After all, if people who work at senior level inside a company are not clear about their core strengths and differentiators, how can they expect the outside world to know? It is sometimes not until companies put their senior people through high-quality media coaching that some of these issues emerge. We sometimes run "message workshops" for organisations trying to work out exactly how they can best define themselves on these issues, what *does* make them stand out. It is very revealing to see quite wide differences emerge, that really should have been ironed out a long time ago – "Oh, I never put it that way, I don't think that sends the right signal, I think we should say it *this* way." Or: "I never looked at it that way; that's a useful way of putting it." Sometimes it really challenges the leadership team to think about these issues and their own strategy in a way they have not done before. These sessions may also generate points that were well known to some parts of the business but not others, and which can be used to strengthen client presentations and other external and internal communications.

What else can you offer?

If the interview is on a reasonably positive topic, such as a business profile or where you are being asked for your opinion on industry issues, think what else you can offer the reporter or interviewer. After all, they are there, eager for material – your direct conduit to their readers, viewers or listeners. The executive with the M-factor will make good use of the opportunity. Do you have any 'lollipops' to offer? That is, nice little points you could make – non-essential but interesting and 'nice to have' – that would help build the relationship, leaving the reporter glad they spoke to you, pleased with the variety of interesting information you have provided. Sometimes they will be self-serving – "By the way, and I don't know if you're already aware of this, but we're very pleased with the way our joint venture in India is going; we've had to adapt to a completely different distribution system over there...," or "This is such a great little gadget, let me show you..." Otherwise, what else could you say that might surprise or interest them? Something counterintuitive perhaps, rather than the same old stuff they have heard many times before? This is the sort of M-factor behaviour that means that the reporter is much more likely to call *you* back next time, rather than someone else on the list.

Other times they are simply positioning you as the 'go-to-guy' for information on the topic or sector, in preference to any of your competition – an opportunity to ensure that it is you who is getting the profile and setting the agenda, rather than someone else. Do you have any background information you can offer – articles or research material? Could you plant an idea for a future article, as in, "By the way, let me know if you're ever doing a piece about changes in planning legislation, because we've got some very strong views on that..." They may not be interested at the time but, one day, under the pressure of deadlines, and needing a quick comment, it is likely to be your name that comes to mind – and they will be very grateful for your help. Build up strong relationships in the good times and they could be invaluable one day.

How to get your point across, even when they haven't asked you

Please do not be like those politicians who come on the radio and say things like, "But that's not important; what *is* important is..." or, "But I'm not here to talk about that, I'm here to talk about..." Bad media trainers tell clients, "Don't worry about the question, whatever he asks just keep saying..." This is not M-factor behaviour. If you come over to the reporter or audience as someone who is defensive or trying to avoid answering legitimate questions, you are unlikely to impress them, whether you tick off your list of key messages or not. If the question asked is completely inappropriate, you do not have to answer it – more on this in chapter 7 – but otherwise, you should be willing to answer the questions if you can, but then be unafraid to move the conversation on to a point you want to make (if that doesn't look like happening naturally).

But how? You want to make it sound as organic and natural as possible. In the trade, they are known as 'bridging phrases', as they help you 'bridge' from one point to another. So in principle it is a matter of ABC – A for Answering (or at least acknowledging) the question; B for Bridging to the point you want to make; and then C for Communicating your message.

If the topic you want to address is linked quite closely to the question that has been asked, it is fairly easy to use a phrase such as, "And that brings me on to...," or "It's the same when..." and to move on to your point. However, you can still achieve the same result even if your topic is quite unrelated to the question. If you feel you have said all you can say or want to say on the topic the reporter is asking about, there is no benefit to either of you in going round in circles. Instead, use a phrase such as, "But it's also worth pointing out that...; or, "And we haven't even touched on the issue of..." or, "What I *do* think is important is..." or just a single word, like 'also' or 'interestingly'. Any of these can lead you to the point you want to make, without annoying the reporter by seeming to not have acknowledged the question. The aim as always is to ensure that both sides go away from the encounter feeling that they have gained something useful. It is advisable to spend some time thinking about exactly which bridging phrases you feel most comfortable with – what sounds good coming from one person's lips can sound forced or unnatural from another's.

As I have pointed out it is often the case that the journalist, who of course rarely knows the topic as well as you, does not always ask the most appropriate or relevant questions – they do not always know what the 'hot button issues' are in your sector. They may be looking for guidance from you as to what is important. So if you have a good key message about your company and its positioning, this will often be informative and helpful rather than annoying. Equally, if they ask a question on an aspect of the topic where you have little to say, a waffly answer, free of specifics, helps neither of you. Better instead to move it on to something you do feel strongly about; a dull question does not have to lead to a dull answer.

Your angle

I have already made the distinction between your core messages and your angle – the main point you want to get across to a journalist with respect to a particular story. The one may be the same as the other, but not necessarily. For instance, let's take a business supplying ethically sourced produce such as cocoa and coffee beans, whose CEO is being interviewed for a profile piece on the company for one of the business sections. The core messages might be:

- *We are one of the country's fastest-growing suppliers of Fairtrade and organic produce. This is a sector with big growth prospects as consumers are increasingly demanding sustainably sourced food, with more flavour and of higher quality.*

- *We are planning the roll-out of a nationwide chain of Fairtrade cafes. Our first three trial branches in London and Manchester are already trading successfully.*

Supposing the CEO later received a call from a journalist writing a news piece about a recent sharp rise in the price of coffee beans. She wants to know how quickly and how far this would be likely to feed through to the consumer in terms of higher prices in the shops. The CEO would still like to get across those same core messages above if he can. But these alone would not be enough. So, in addition, his *angles* on this occasion might be:

- *We do believe that there is no option but to pass on some of these price increases to consumers. We will keep these down as far as possible, but we do believe raw coffee prices have been unsustainably low for a long time and producers need higher prices in order to be able to survive, so this is something customers will have to accept.*

- *Higher prices are inevitable in the longer term to give a better deal to producers, but we have made a pledge to keep prices at their current level in our new Fairtrade cafe chain for at least three months. Rising prices will not affect our plans to roll out the chain nationwide over the next three years.*

So on this occasion the CEO has a total of four key messages he would like to get across. He knows his angle on the need for price rises may not be popular with everybody, but it is aligned to his company's culture and market positioning. He also knows this comment is likely to differentiate his business from other suppliers, and may therefore be more quotable. For example, it is unlikely the reporter will have had this response if she called up one of the big supermarket chains. The CEO has also used the interview as an opportunity to make the reporter aware of the plan for the new chain of cafes, and with any luck get a plug for them.

To know what you want to say, you need to understand what the reporter is looking for. You need to be clear in your own mind about the reporter's agenda, and make sure you have a couple of interesting points to make so that if at all possible he or she goes away feeling it was worth calling you. So whoever handles incoming media enquiries on your behalf should find out what publication the reporter is calling from, who the readership is (if this is not obvious), and what their own 'angle' is – in other words, what is the reporter's approach to the story. If it is a negative angle then they may not want to give too much away so you will have to use common sense and be prepared for a trickier conversation. You will rarely get a complete list of questions, although sometimes reporters will flood you with emails covering every conceivable angle. You should certainly know enough about the question areas to decide what you want to get across.

Key Reminders

■ *Before you start talking to the media, establish your organisation's core messages, if you have not already done so. Look for opportunities to get these across when appropriate.*

■ *Think how you would like a journalist to position you and your business in print – if you don't know, you can't expect them to. Be clear about what makes you stand out from the competition.*

■ *Consistency is important – it never impresses journalists when the left hand of an organisation seems to have little knowledge of what the right hand is up to.*

■ *Try to have a particular angle on the story the reporter is putting together – a specific viewpoint rather than a woolly response. This is more helpful to reporters and makes them more likely to seek your views in future.*

■ *When you have a reporter's attention, think what else you could offer him or her that could be of interest; you might be able to plant an interesting angle for future use.*

■ *Use bridging phrases if necessary to help you move the conversation on to the points you want to make, once you have dealt with the question asked.*

Chapter 6

Style and tone

Body language can be important

Style and tone

In earlier chapters, I have touched on the fact that when you are communicating to the media, as much as to clients or customers, style and tone – in other words how you say it – are just as important as what you say. This is a key element of the M-factor. Away from the pressure of a crisis, you want the reporter or the television or radio audience to like you, or at least to take you seriously. Otherwise, why should they listen to you? Ask people you trust for some honest feedback here – do you come over as hectoring or irritable at times, or as cold and unfriendly when you are feeling under pressure? These are not the impressions you want to leave when you do a media interview.

Building believability and trust

Certainly if you want to sell people something, or persuade them of something, or otherwise raise your profile in a positive way, you do need them to warm to you. In interviews it comes down to those indefinable qualities that we are all looking for when we meet someone for the first time, or see them interviewed on television. Do I feel I like or respect this person? Do I feel I believe what they are telling me? Would I trust them? Do they seem to be authentic, rather than phony? We all subconsciously make these sorts of analyses to come to a gut feeling about what we think of somebody. They all need to be there as part of the M-factor.

Believability and trust come about through being open and honest in your communication, coming across as someone who is genuinely dealing with the issue rather than someone who is 'spinning'. If you are too 'on-message', never really answering the question, that will be seen as counterproductive – it can be very frustrating to a journalist trying to get to the heart of the matter. Similarly, I meet people whose tactic is usually to try to 'close down' the interview as quickly as they can when a journalist calls, viewing them as an irritant, and with the objective of saying as little as possible so as not to get themselves into trouble. This is never going to help them get the media coverage they desire.

Recently, there has been much talk about the need for organisations to have transparency in what they do, in order to restore the levels of trust in big companies. If you appear to be in denial about a problem in your business or industry, for instance, that is likely to call into question the credibility of any of the other points you have made. If you are defensive, people will tend to assume that you know you are guilty, but dare not admit it. By contrast, if you are clear about what you want to say, and believe in what you are planning to say, then it is more likely that a sense of confidence, openness and honesty will be conveyed in your whole style and approach in the interview – and that you will get the reporter and audience on-side.

The ultimate objective is to build long-term relationships with the main journalists and media outlets in your sector. This can be of huge benefit; next time you have something you want to say to the media, it is a lot easier if you are already on first-name terms with journalists and can pick up the phone and call them. It also means you have some 'credit in the bank' in a crisis – if you have helped that reporter in the past they are likely to have some sympathy for you, and are more likely to cut you some slack in the difficult times. This is why it is important to leave them with positive feelings towards you if you possibly can.

If you meet a reporter face to face, think about your body language. Try to engage in an open, friendly style – do not talk to them with a frown on your face, your arms folded, or in any other way that sends a 'keep away' signal. It is acknowledged that this is not always easy, particularly if you find that you are talking but the journalist is busy making notes and so does not make eye contact with you, but you should try where possible to keep positive, friendly interaction at the fore. Again, it can be useful to ask for candid feedback from those close to you. Do you have irritating habits or nervous vocal tics? Do you tend to stare at the ceiling when replying to awkward questions? Put these right if you can, or at least be aware of them so you can minimise their impact.

Your 'hinterland'

If you are viewed by journalists as a 'product guy' or a 'marketing woman' they are unlikely to be interested in whose suits you wear, or what you do at the weekends, or what you think about the long-term future of the industry. But if you are seen as, or want to be seen as, a 'leader', then these things can come into play, particularly if your status is such that you become the subject of the occasional business feature about you or the company. Then, such issues as the company culture become relevant, and the tone is usually set by the person at the top.

Should you be in this category, or heading there, think about your 'back story' and how you want to position yourself. Family man or working mum, juggling business meetings with the need to be at the school sports day? Aggressive go-getter, extreme sports fan, work-hard–play-hard, ultra-competitive in everything you do? Thoughtful intellectual, with valuable big-picture insights that your competitors aren't smart enough to match? Top-flight change manager, with a passion to transform the organisation? Down-to-earth individual who worked their way from the shop floor right to the top? Journalists love to be able to categorise, but at the same time they are always looking for those unexpected human touches that make you more interesting, so they can get a 'handle' on what you are all about.

For this type of longer-form interview, you should think about exactly what picture you want to paint about yourself, rather than leave the reporter to come up with something that may not be aligned to the way you see yourself at all – that in fact could be damaging. I remember reading a profile piece on the boss of a medium-sized law firm. The journalist obviously did not think that the gentleman had much of interest to say, and a fair chunk of the end article was devoted to a discussion of how the interview subject had gradually crushed his polystyrene cup during the course of the conversation, and then absentmindedly ripped it up into tiny pieces, indicating (in the reporter's eyes) a distracted nature and discomfort with his role.

If there are elements you would rather the reporter did *not* focus on, be generic and not very interesting in what you say on these, and with luck the reporter will probably move on. By contrast, be much more vivid, enthusiastic and quotable on things you *are* happy to be quoted on. There are forks in every conversation; try to lead yours in the more appropriate, relevant and useful directions, not the awkward ones. If you are somewhat generic about everything, do not expect to be happy with the outcome. You want the reporter to come away thinking 'interesting woman' or 'interesting guy' rather than, "Well I didn't get much out of that." For the M-factor, you have to play your part and give the journalist material to show them you *are* worth keeping in touch with.

So a workable strategy may be to find two or three things about yourself that you *are* happy to share, that you can always pull out if a reporter wants to find out a bit more about your 'hinterland'. Your biggest business influence? A childhood event that shaped your attitude? The challenge you had to overcome? The biggest business mistake you ever made and what you learned from it? An unusual hobby? A passion for an obscure sports team? They are all things that will give the reporter an insight on what makes you tick, and stop them tearing their hair out because you have come over as unexceptional and 'plain vanilla'. Currently popular with some publications is the quick-fire Q&A designed to elicit a telling insight on character, such as, 'Madonna or Mozart? Suntan or skiing?' It is not a bad idea to think how you may wish to position yourself on the elitist–populist axis.

Style and tone when under pressure

If you are giving a 'responsibility' interview (see chapter 2) and there are difficult issues to deal with, try not to let the pressure inside you show on the outside. Remember, many journalists will employ the devil's advocate approach, to put you on the spot and see if you have a convincing line of response. It doesn't mean they will necessarily attack you in print – as long as you have given a good account of yourself. In fact I have spoken to many people who have dreaded the appearance of a certain article, because the reporter sounded so fearsome on the phone – and who have then been pleasantly surprised at the outcome. Conversely, others specialise in sounding sweet and reasonable when they talk to you, and then put the boot in, in print. Your best tactic is to be consistently pleasant. Be friendly to journalists even if they are not.

As mentioned earlier, other reporters use the tactic of silence – saying nothing at all when you have delivered your answer, perhaps in the hope you will add more to what you have already said, thereby giving more away than you meant to. You should not let yourself be pressured in this way; it is up to them to come up with further questions if they want to. Better still, after a pause for thought if need be, continue the interview by moving on yourself to one of the points you want to make.

Often we tend to 'mirror' the person we are with in terms of style, tone, body language and speed of speech. Be aware of this, and try to do so only if this is going to help you. For instance, if the journalist is talking very fast, it does not mean you automatically have to do the same yourself. You do not have to rush in with immediate responses to counter a negative point he or she has raised, conveying the impression you are irritated or angry. Keep calm, take a pause for breath and speak at a steady rather than a fast pace. How do you expect a journalist to accurately report you if you go so fast they cannot get your words down? Allow yourself some breathing space; this will also give you more time to think and will add more weight and authority to what you say. Instead of being reactive, put yourself back in control.

Style and tone when meeting journalists informally

Occasionally you may find yourself meeting journalists in informal situations, as opposed to situations when they are calling you or meeting you for a specific interview. The way you behave then should be friendly and hospitable, rather than wary, on the basis that you might get caught out saying something you shouldn't.

PRs sometimes invite influential journalists to hospitality events in order to help them 'get to know' clients better, thereby creating the opportunity for better relationships to be built in relaxed circumstances. These are not appropriate occasions for heavy agenda setting, as this may be counterproductive if the reporter had expected some off-duty relaxation and free drinks. Remember, you want them to like you, and the objective should be more about long-term relationship building. However, you should always have a few points ready to make if the occasion arises, and expect to be ready to answer informal questions. Reporters are like broadband – 'always on'. They are constantly on the lookout for a story, and will often see this situation as an opportunity to chat to you about how business is going, what you think about developments in the market, competitor activity, and so on. Journalists will not normally assume that your words on these occasions are for attribution, but if the conversation starts to get interesting, they will not be able to forget what you have said. Do not fall into the trap of assuming everything is 'off the record', enabling you to be as rude as you like about everybody in your industry. This stuff may be too good for them to ignore.

In these circumstances, do not be too bland, but at least be diplomatic – you should still think about what your words would look like on the page. Instead of describing a competitor product as 'useless', 'rubbish', or 'a complete dog', you might – with a wry smile on your face – say it is 'an interesting approach'. Then, instead of getting bogged down in detail, you might go on to say, "Our approach is different – we feel it's more important to..." Then you have made your views clear, but without any incriminating quotes, and you are back in the comfort zone on what your own company is doing. If it starts getting intense, and you feel you are suddenly being interviewed instead of having an informal chat, it is better to say, in a friendly manner, something like, "Look, if you want to chat in detail about this, I'm happy to speak, but this probably isn't the right time – give me a call in the morning and we'll see if we can fix something up."

Sometimes, after the influence of a little alcohol, people can get carried away and behave badly, or say things they shouldn't. As host, try to stay one or two drinks behind your guests. You do not want the event to result in some unfortunate comments in one of the diary or gossip columns, or on some scandal-mongering website. With the press around, you are never 'off-duty'.

If you are meeting a reporter or group of reporters for a lunch that has been organised by you or your PR, you should make the status of the conversation clear at the beginning, to avoid misunderstandings. If nothing is said about this, a journalist may legitimately assume everything is on the record. If you feel this will inhibit the free flow of conversation, say right at the beginning, "I hope it's OK with everyone if we keep this on a background basis? If there is anything you do want to quote, have a word with me afterwards and we'll make sure we give you something." Again, the style is friendly but clear and professional.

Key Reminders

■ *Believability and trust are at least as important as your message. If you come across as defensive, reporters and television and radio audiences may instinctively feel you are guilty in some way, or hiding something.*

■ *Think about your body language if you meet a journalist face to face. Try to communicate in an open, friendly style.*

■ *If you are the subject of a 'profile piece' where you are the story, you need to be able to talk about a lot more than just a few key messages. Think about what impression you might create, including how you would like to come across in broad terms, inside and outside of the office.*

■ *In difficult circumstances, ensure you remain as patient, friendly and polite as possible with journalists, even if they are asking difficult or aggressive questions and are not courteous themselves.*

■ *Try to speak more slowly rather than rushing through. This gives you time to think, can make you sound more deliberate and authoritative, and will give the reporter more time to absorb and jot down accurately what you are saying.*

■ *If you meet journalists in an informal situation, remember they are still instinctively on the lookout for a story – try to have a few interesting titbits for them. Do not assume everything is off the record; if you are indiscreet your comments may be too good for some reporters to ignore.*

Chapter 7

Dealing with difficult questions

In a spin: the 'CEO Triple Salchow'

FACTOR

Dealing with difficult questions

Everybody who has to deal with the media is worried about what will happen if they get asked a question they are unable to answer. The fear of failure is powerful – the fear of making a complete fool of oneself, or causing great damage to the business by saying something injudicious, even more so. So what are the best prevention and coping strategies?

The first thing is to be realistic about how the media are likely to view you and your organisation. Do not be in denial about your issues. Clearly, the chief executive of a quoted company can expect to be under pressure if revenues and profits are falling without solid external reasons, particularly if his pay has gone up substantially in the last year or two. It is easy to make predictions as to the approach a journalist might take. By contrast, a small business being forced to lay off workers because of a downturn in the economy can reasonably expect a more sympathetic hearing, as this will probably be categorised by the reporter as a 'victim' interview rather than a 'responsibility' interview.

The key, therefore, is to anticipate what are likely to be the sensitive issues, and have lines of response prepared in case they come up. You can never think of every single possible question and angle so do not even worry about trying; instead of becoming bogged down in the wording of the questions you should focus more on the underlying issues and what exactly you want to say about them. So whenever that key word or phrase comes from the reporter's mouth, you should be ready with a response already pretty fully formed in your mind, even before he or she has finished phrasing the question. You can then adapt it as appropriate to the specific question asked.

Use your media relations team or external PR advisers to brainstorm possible tricky issues; they can help you come up with lines of response. Journalists often see things in very black and white terms. It makes it much easier to write the story if it is clear to the reader who is the hero and who is the villain in the tale. You cannot turn a black into a white, but you should be able to make the reporter realise that the issues are probably a lot less clearcut than they imagined – much more of a shade of grey. You may not be happy if the story turns out 75% negative with only 25% positive, but that is a lot better than 100% negative.

During media training sessions a lot of people ask me whether reporters have frequently made up their mind already what they are going to write, even before carrying out the interview. The answer is that while in many circumstances they will be open-minded, it is true that this will not always be the case. Take a reporter who has been told by his or her editor something like, "I want 1,000 words on why the bankers are to blame for the financial crisis." The reporter is not going to be very open-minded at all, knowing full well what that editor is looking for.

You have to be realistic about this. Does it mean that if you think you are not going to get a very fair hearing, you should avoid the encounter and refuse to talk? This will always be a matter of judgment. The danger is that if you are a bank in these circumstances and you are willing to defend your corner to the publication while others go to ground, you may become the focus of attention for criticism, while others escape scot-free.

So this approach is very understandable, when no one organisation feels itself responsible for defending an attack on a whole sector. However, the danger is that when everybody behaves this way, the criticism of bankers (in this case) becomes that much fiercer, as there is nobody to put their side of the argument, and they are portrayed as extremely defensive – guilty in the minds of readers and viewers. If at all possible, therefore, it is better when under attack to face the music, patiently and doggedly explaining your position and making your counter-arguments as reasonably as possible – but you had better have some good answers prepared that will deal with the criticism effectively. If the attacks are being levelled at your company in particular, you will be painted in an extremely negative light if you are not willing to account for yourself on a matter of public interest. So you need to line up your defence.

This is not a matter of spin – at least it shouldn't be. It is a matter of foreseeing each potential challenge, and working out your best line of response to it. As I have said, you cannot predict every possible way a question might be framed, but you and your media advisers should be able to identify the key lines of criticism and work out what to put across on each. The key advice here is to resist the temptation to lie. You will rarely if ever tell the whole truth – that applies if I ask you something innocuous like, "Did you have a good weekend?" or, "Why did you decide to launch this product at this time?" So it will be no different if you get asked a tricky question – there are nearly always multiple reasons why an organisation does what it does, and not all of them will be for public consumption. But what you say should be true – and that does not mean telling a half truth that is designed to mislead. Too many politicians over the past twenty years have become used to spinning their way through a web of half truths, which have earned the whole lot of them an extremely bad name. I do not believe it can be in your long-term interests, even if facing tough issues, to take this route.

For example, fans of the US television drama *The West Wing* will be familiar with the 'non-denial denial'. This is something designed to make it look as if you are saying one thing, while the opposite is true – without lying. Thus, a politician under attack may criticise his opponents for 'talking rubbish'. The aim here is to make it look as if the allegations are being denied, but he hasn't actually quite said they have no truth in them. An innocuous, non-political example came from *3rd Rock from the Sun* actor Joseph Gordon-Levitt in 2012. When asked by *The Times* if, after appearing in the latest blockbuster *Batman* movie, he was being lined up to become the next Batman himself, he answered, "You know, I think it's wonderful how passionate people are about this movie... and that's great. But that doesn't mean any of it's true." A great non-denial denial, all in the spirit of keeping the public guessing. However, if you are setting out deliberately to mislead on a serious issue, this sort of thing nearly always gets found out in the end, and it usually makes you look a lot worse than if you had 'fessed up' in the first place. In the court of public opinion, you may find you get a lot more credit for honesty than you may have expected.

In general I advise against getting bogged down in trying to create and memorise long Q&A documents. They can sometimes be useful as an exercise to think through the potential lines a reporter might take, but in my experience they are not only impossible to memorise, but in practice the questions come up differently anyway. It is usually better to extract the essence from the Q&A and boil it down to a small number of key messages. Ensure these are as powerful as possible, backed up by your best evidence from the EQuALS formula. You can use the power of repetition so that they come over loud and clear, and the reporter cannot claim they missed the point. Think about whatever you can say that will, if appropriate, put the matter in context without being defensive, or evading the central issue.

Seven techniques you can use

1   Say what you can say

The tendency when under fire is to worry about all the things you can't say, that you don't want to talk about. Instead focus on the legitimate points you are able to make. For example, there may be non-time-specific points you can get across that remain as true when under pressure as they were previously – such as, "I can't give you those figures, but the point I would make is..." or, "As I have explained, we have what we believe are the strictest safety standards in the industry." Not great perhaps, but better than nothing.

2   Explain what you can't say

There will be times when you are tempted just to say "no comment". Tempting, but in fact more likely to lead to you being portrayed as the villain of the piece. Do you really want stories in the paper along the lines of "The finance director of Megacorp has refused to comment on industry reports of a massive black hole in the accounts, blamed on..." Even if there is no substance to the suggestion, everyone will assume that things are really bad – if the reports hadn't been true, presumably you would have denied them. After all, goes the argument, there is no smoke without fire. If there really is a good reason why you cannot give a particular answer, then explain it and the reporter will normally understand. Commercially sensitive? Market sensitive? A confidentiality agreement in place? They could all be legitimate reasons why you do not want to part with a specific piece of information, and all are better than "no comment".

3   Pass it on

You may be concerned about negative issues that are in fact the responsibility of others within the organisation. In that case, leave it to them. You can quite legitimately say something such as, "That's not something I've been involved with. You would need to talk to the offshore division on that," or, "If you speak to the media relations department, they will be able to help you a lot more than I can." It is not a case of evading the question; it is about ensuring that the best-informed and most appropriate person is dealing with the matter, not someone who is unlikely to be in possession of all the facts.

4   Call back later

Often you will be asked for facts that you cannot reel off from the top of your head. It is possible to get quite defensive in these circumstances, feeling you are letting the side down. Do not make the mistake of assuming that the reporter had previously imagined you to be somehow omnipotent, being in possession of all the possible information on a topic. Better to be quite open. Rather than apologising too much and conveying your awkwardness, just say something like, "I don't have those figures right in front of me, but I'll do what I can to dig them out, and I'll come back to you." You have bought yourself more thinking time – and the reporter would generally prefer the right answer in fifteen minutes rather than the wrong answer now. But do follow through.

5   Put it in context

If I hear a politician on the radio or television starting his or her answer with, "Let me put that in context", I always tend to assume that they are going to avoid dealing with the issue, by sidetracking so much that by the time they have finished talking we will have forgotten what the question was. So the phrase can be a red rag to a bull. Having said that, context is vital; a motivated journalist can make almost any slip-up sound unforgivable if we take it on its own. For example, "Surely that processing failure suggests that your organisation is completely incompetent?" might be a leading question from an aggressive journalist. But the overall picture may be rather different. It should be pretty reasonable on your part to point out, "We are very disappointed that the error crept in, and we apologise to those affected. We are currently reviewing and upgrading our systems to reduce the error rate still further – but it's important to bear in mind that we process several million trades every month, and of these the number with problems can be counted on the fingers of one hand."

6 Don't be led by leading questions

Imagine your organisation is under attack and a reporter suggests to you, "Isn't it true to say this has become a nightmare for your customers, and a disaster for your corporate reputation?" If you respond, "I wouldn't say this is a disaster for us, but clearly it has caused some problems for our customers," these words can be quoted against you. You have allowed the reporter to frame the debate purely in terms of how much of a 'disaster' or 'nightmare' it is. You should use the language *you* believe to be most appropriate. Instead of repeating the negative words, find something that conveys what positive steps you are taking to deal with the issue, as in, "Our team are working extremely hard to ensure..."

7 Stick to your line

A persistent reporter may find several ways of coming back to the same issue, to try to get you to say more than you had perhaps planned. This is where a lot of people come unstuck in interviews – under the impression that what they have said has not been adequate, they feel obliged to add just a bit more in the hope of making it OK. Of course, this simply gives the journalist the incentive to push a bit harder, as they can see their persistence paying off. So if you are clear in your own mind that your answer was a fair one the first time, then stick to your guns and do not be afraid to repeat it. You may use different words but essentially you are demonstrating that you won't be pushed around. Once again, however, I should stress that your first answer does always need to deal with the matter in hand. If it is a 'responsibility' interview then make sure you have a solid answer prepared – if it is a weak one, its inadequacies will be increasingly exposed as the reporter persists.

You also have to demonstrate politeness and confidence. Try saying to yourself, "There's really not a lot I can add to that," in an angry, agitated voice. Now think what impression that is likely to leave with the reporter – someone who is angry, defensive, irritable and stressed. This is likely to be reflected in the finished article. Now try saying the same words but with a warm smile on your face – as if you were talking to a friend who had asked you about some entertaining gossip you felt it better not to go into. You have, with any luck, created a very different impression: someone who is firm but patient, friendly and human. As ever, style and tone do matter.

There are questions you don't have to answer

You are not in a court of law, under oath, when you are being interviewed, and you may feel there are questions you do not need to answer. If the information is client-confidential, or market-sensitive, for instance, do not be defensive, as I have said. Use a phrase such as, "I don't have those figures but..." and then use a bridging word or phrase to move on to something that *is* in the public domain that you would like to get across. However, there are also other types of question that you should not feel obliged to answer.

Hypothetical questions

Purely hypothetical questions are usually of little benefit to you but can lead to a whole lot of trouble. There are many voices in the media willing to speculate about everything from England football results to interest rate decisions by the world's central banks. Breakfast television and radio news shows in particular like to be especially 'forward looking' as opposed to 'backward looking' – in other words, rather than just rehashing the news from the previous night, they like to look forward to the expected events of the day.

This all means reporters will often try to get interviewees to surmise on matters. It can be a perfectly reasonable thing to ask for, but where possible you should try to avoid answering questions that are purely hypothetical – it is far too easy for a quote to be used against you. So if an interviewer asks, "What if *this* event occurs?" or, "What if *that* event?" then a warning bell should sound in your head. We often hit clients with these "what-ifs" in our media training courses, and people are often surprised at how easily they fall into the trap.

Let's look at an example: an expert on house prices was sent to work with us some years ago after some negative experiences with reporters. He had been asked by a newspaper journalist about his views on the property outlook in a difficult economic climate. His view was not a controversial one at the time: he said that house prices were likely to rise by up to 5% over the coming year, as long as there weren't any big economic shocks.

The reporter was looking for something a little more sensational, however. "So you're saying that if there's a sharp interest rate rise then we could be facing another crash in house prices?" he asked. The journalist is always looking for a good headline when interviewing people, and knows that a warning of a house price crash in the area will be of interest to the editor, and might even make the front page. "Well, if there were to be a sudden large rise in interest rates then, yes, that would mean a big downturn in the market," said our man – or words along those lines. The reporter had found his story.

Our expert had been sucked into the trap of talking about an unlikely hypothetical situation. "Of course I don't think there's much, if any likelihood of that happening," he added, but by then it was too late. The story appeared with a headline full of talk of "local expert warns of house price crash" or similar. The commentator was not predicting this at all, but the uninformed newspaper reader would not be aware of that.

I should emphasise that not all print media journalists are as willing as the one in this example to take the story beyond its reasonable boundaries that way – but some will. You should make sure you do not fall into the trap, and it would have been easy to avoid the predicament in this case. The property expert could have said, "In fact, I don't forecast any sharp rise in interest rates over the coming year. That is only likely to occur if the economy really speeds ahead, taking house prices with it, and there isn't any obvious sign of that at the moment. What I think is much more likely is..." If you want to speculate, try to keep the focus on likely outcomes and realistic events – not on unlikely hypotheticals that may create an entirely incorrect impression.

Personal questions

If you are having a quick phone conversation with a reporter, giving views on the market you operate in, your personal life should be of little or no consequence. If, by contrast, you are the CEO and it is a longer conversation as part of a magazine feature about your company, then you yourself will be much more central to the story. Reporters in this situation may want to know not just your age, but whether or not you are married with children, where you live, what your hobbies are and what your formative influences were. They are looking for something that will provide an insight into what makes you tick as an individual, in the hope that it will give colour to the piece and interest their readers. They do not usually know what it is until they hear it – so these types of questions can sometimes be a 'fishing expedition', carried out until they feel they have something that will characterise you effectively and strike a chord with their readers.

You may feel that some of these very personal questions are impertinent, or that they invade your privacy. For instance, most people would feel uncomfortable being asked questions about what they are paid. If this is public knowledge through the report and accounts, there is no point in hiding it; otherwise, however, it may be enough to use a generic phrase such as, "I think I'm paid reasonably for the job I am doing," or, "I think my compensation is competitive but pretty much in line with the market." Again, do not be defensive; move the conversation on when you have said as much as you feel you can.

Many people who have moved up in the corporate world feel with some justification that their families deserve their privacy and should not become 'part of the story'. This is more than understandable, but there are two issues here. First, many people have already made huge amounts of information about themselves public through social media websites such as Facebook and LinkedIn. Think what is already out there about you, waiting for a reporter to pick up? You may have set your privacy settings fairly conservatively, but have your friends? There is no point in getting upset about a publication 'invading your privacy' if you have already comprehensively done the job yourself.

Second, once you have made a comment to a reporter and it gets printed, you cannot un-say it. In a digital era you should assume that any information you have given may be searchable. Once privacy has been breached, it is hard to reassert it. I advise clients who may find themselves in this situation to think carefully about some points that they are happy to share, so they at least have *something* to give a reporter who is simply trying to do his or her job by making you sound more interesting. If you stonewall on everything, do not be surprised if you are portrayed as controlling and defensive. You may come over as very reasonable, however, if you say something like, "I have a couple of teenage children, but I prefer to allow them to keep their privacy – however I suppose that beyond the family, my passion has always been..."

Key Reminders

◼ *Be realistic about how positively or negatively the journalist is likely to view you. Hope for the best but be prepared for the worst, just in case. Reporters may or may not be open-minded.*

◼ *Anticipate any sensitive issues that may be brought up and work out your most effective lines of response, with evidence to back up your case.*

◼ *Know your boundaries – if a journalist asks about something that is not your responsibility, pass it on where possible to the appropriate person for response.*

◼ *Avoid saying "no comment" when asked about a difficult issue, as it makes you look guilty. If you can, give reasons as to why you may not be able to fully answer the reporter's questions.*

◼ *If you do not have the information to hand to answer a question, it is perfectly reasonable to explain you need to double-check, and to then call the journalist back after establishing the facts.*

◼ *If a journalist is persistent, but you feel you have answered the question as fully as you can, stick to your guns – politely – rather than allow yourself to be pressured into saying more than you should.*

◼ *You do not have to answer hypothetical or inappropriate personal questions.*

Chapter 8

Preparing to be great on television and radio

Confidence comes from being well-prepared

FACTOR

Preparing to be great on television and radio

Once, a television appearance seemed a remote possibility for the majority of business people, but with the multiplication of channels via cable, satellite and the internet, that is no longer the case. In very broad-brush terms, I would think of three levels of opportunity. At the top level there are national, mass-market broadcast channels, no longer as dominant as they were, but still talking in audiences of millions, rather than hundreds or thousands; included here would be BBC1, Channel 4, ITV and so on in the UK, ABC, NBC in the US, and their equivalents. This is the 'general public' – anything you say has to be understood by the man or woman next door, your aunt, cousin or granny. No business jargon here. M-factor behaviour involves thinking about who your audience is, and how to pitch what you say in the most appropriate way, so your message is more likely to resonate.

At the next level come the specialist and local channels – a much smaller audience but potentially very powerful for communicating to specific target markets, such as market-savvy investors who may see you on CNBC or Bloomberg; or people living in Baltimore, Adelaide or north-east England who may see your company on the relevant local news. These outlets tend to be hungry for content, and very beneficial if their target market is also yours.

At the third level are the more niche broadcast and online channels and websites. Subscribers on satellite systems such as Sky or STAR TV (Satellite Television Asian Region) can view whole channels devoted to country pursuits, weddings, fitness, fashion and so on. Every trade magazine has a website, and most if not all of these sites now carry video as well as text content. They may be seen by relatively small numbers of people, but remember that the content may stay online for months or years. Over time, those numbers add up, so do not dismiss these outlets out of hand. If nothing else, they can be relationship-building opportunities, and can provide a chance to practise your television skills, so that if BBC News comes knocking at your door, you are more likely to feel familiar with the process. For more on creating your own online video content, see chapter 10.

Nearly everything I have said in earlier chapters about the media mindset, and the art of the good quote or soundbite, applies as much to broadcast as to interviews with the written media; the interviewers are still journalists, and think the same, but the message reaches people in a different way. Here, however, you have to focus not only on the material, but on the delivery. No actor would expect to go on stage in front of a few hundred people without a lot of rehearsal – yet I have come across many people that will assume they can do a radio or television interview that may be seen by hundreds of thousands, or even millions of people, just by sitting down and doing their best to answer some questions off the top of their head. This is risky to say the least – it is where good media training comes in, giving you focus, practice, and helping you get the performance element right. Do ensure you give yourself enough time to rehearse, rather than expecting to 'wing it'.

Another key difference is that whereas a newspaper or magazine journalist will process your material, ensuring that it is pitched at the right level for the readers, with broadcast you are talking direct to the audience. So you will have to work a bit harder to ensure you are hitting the target – expunge the jargon from your vocabulary, use everyday language rather than business-speak, and make broad-brush points rather than precise ones; for instance, you might say 'three-quarters' rather than '73.6 %'.

Seven key questions to ask before you are interviewed on television/radio

Even more than with interviews with 'print' media journalists, the key is to make sure you know, as far as possible, what you are letting yourself in for. Your media advisers or PR agency will normally ask some key questions before they put you forward. These apply to both radio and television.

1 Who is the audience?

There is obviously a very big difference in style between a local television interview and something for a business channel, or for children's television. You want to make sure you fit in, and that you know what is expected. Be realistic. If your company is involved in a dirty or controversial industry, and you get a call from a show with a history of investigative reporting, do not expect you are there for a bit of chit-chat; you should be prepared for a real grilling. Understand so far as you can what role you are likely to play in the broadcast – victim, expert, or perhaps villain? There are times when there is mud flying about that it is probably sensible to stand back and try not to get involved if possible – take the advice of your PR experts. However, if you are the target of complaints or allegations, it is nearly always better to show up and put your side of the story, rather than to try to hide in the hope no one will notice. You could be vilified, yet you have turned down the chance to answer back. You have to do it well though, and this requires serious media training. If you do it badly that will make things much worse.

2 What is their angle?

Nobody ever asks someone to give an interview just for the sake of it; there is always a reason why they are suddenly interested in that particular topic on that particular day. The more you understand what is motivating them, the more likely you are to be able to anticipate what sort of questions are likely to come up.

3 What are the question areas?

You might get a list of questions, but it will very rarely be a complete list, because a lot of the questions you will be asked will depend on your earlier responses, and what the reporter wants to follow up. But you need to be clear that you are the right person, in the right place, at the right time, with a clear idea of what they are expecting.

4 What is the style of interview?

You want to know if you are being interviewed on your own, or as part of a broader discussion, with other contributors. Is it just a quick two or three minute slot, where you need to get your points across as quickly as possible, or something more substantial, in which case you might want to pace yourself very differently? Is it a serious business show, or is at aimed at a much broader general audience? You should pitch your replies accordingly. If you are appearing on radio, the style of the show will often be very much driven by the style of the host – some are deliberately provocative or play it for laughs. It is normally best in these circumstances to mirror the style if you can. If the format is informal and chatty, you will be expected to sing for your supper and provide a good level of entertainment value. The more you can make the host look good, the more they are likely to reciprocate and make you look good.

5   What are the practicalities?

For radio, this may involve travelling to the studio, or simply talking by phone from your home or office. For television, it may be a lot more elaborate. Do they want you to come to the studio or are they coming to you? If the latter, they may be looking for additional filming opportunities – some pictures to cover their script. What could you provide for them, over and above some dull shots of people sitting at their computers? If you can be creative and come up with some interesting or attractive visuals, the end result is likely to be a lot better. But be aware that it may take a lot longer for them to shoot these visuals than you may expect. It is not usually just a case of a quick 'point and shoot' – it may involve lighting and the direction of some quite elaborate sequences in some cases. This can be time-consuming and may involve some business disruption. Try to get a realistic estimate of what is likely to be involved. For television you should also be aware of the difference between a face-to-face interview and one where you are 'down the line', or contributing from a remote location; in the latter case you may feel a bit cut off from the action – you have to talk directly into the camera, treating it like a person, usually hearing your questions through an earpiece. For most people this takes some training and practice to do comfortably.

6   Is the interview going to be pre-recorded... ?

The advantage of a pre-recorded interview is that if you make a mess of one of your responses, you can have another go. If you realise you are going down the wrong track in one of your answers, it is better to stop and start again at the beginning; that always works much better for the producer than trying to do a clunky edit. There are two ways your pre-recorded interview can be used, and they can make a big difference in how you appear, so you should always ask about their intentions. The first and perhaps most common way is when the reporter goes round and interviews various different people, using a little sliver of each interview – known as a 'soundbite'. He or she will put these with a scripted commentary. On television these chunks of commentary will be covered by pictures, to make up the typical 'reporter package' that you see on the television news. What that means is that, out of your whole interview, which might last between five and twenty minutes, the broadcasters will perhaps use only one or two little fifteen-second comments. It is very hard for you to know quite which bit they are going to pick, so it is important to be prepared to repeat your key points several times, giving them various different options as to how they use the points you most want to make but making it abundantly clear what you think is most important.

The other type of pre-recorded interview is when it is being recorded "as live'; here the team records an interview and plays back all or part of it through from beginning to end for broadcast. It is easier for them, requires less editing, and is more appropriate for certain types of broadcast output. Then, of course, it is more like a normal conversation, so you should not keep repeating the same point quite so many times over. It is best to imagine as far as you can that this really is 'live', and you should aim to get right through it without retakes so far as possible, otherwise you may lose the flow and become embarrassed at your lack of eloquence.

7 ... or will it be live?

The advantage of a live interview is that the broadcaster cannot unfairly edit you, perhaps taking the very snippet that positions you in a controversial light and leaving out all the parts you thought were important. With a live interview, what you say is what the audience gets. That is why a lot of politicians prefer this option, because they know that if they *appear, they can make their particular point and know it will be broadcast. For a lot of people, of course, 'live' feels scary. If you have never done an interview before, pre-recorded may be preferable if you get that opportunity offered, because at least you have the chance to have another go should nerves get the better of you. Once you get more proficient and confident, the live experience will probably not be as bad as you fear, and the extra adrenaline may well help you to a sharper, livelier performance. Anyway, you do not usually get a choice.*

The pre-interview chat

In most cases the producer or interviewer will want to speak to you directly beforehand, to find out what sort of points you are likely to make – unless you are already a well-known figure, in which case they will take what they can get. This pre-interview chat is vital, unless you are highly experienced – you can get a feel and a flavour of their approach, and suggest issues you would like to raise that they might not otherwise have thought of. If necessary you can work to reduce expectations of how much you will be able to say on any sensitive aspects of the topic; it is about managing expectations on both sides. Once you have extracted as much information as you can, you need to get your thoughts together in the same way as for a conversation with a journalist working with the written word. You now know what sorts of questions are likely to be raised and can think about what you want to say, and what your objectives are for the interview. You can also make an educated guess at any 'dreaded questions' that may be coming up. Rehearse your main points so they trip off your tongue – you do not want to be hunting for the right words in the interview itself.

Hair, makeup, clothing

Before a studio television interview, whether pre-recorded or live, you may be offered makeup – you should always take it. It is a good idea to avoid a naked face. Even a dusting of powder from a compact is better than nothing, as it will take the 'shine' off under the lights. This is especially important under harsh studio lighting, but not a bad idea on location as well, at least indoors when lights have been set up. Do not be embarrassed to ask, particularly if you are someone who tends to perspire or 'shine'. Women should wear a thicker layer of foundation than they might normally, as it will make the skin look smoother, and stop you looking faded. Not all channels have a permanent makeup person on call, so it is best to bring your own just in case, and give yourself time to get it applied properly. The female presenters on many channels now have thick makeup that is applied through a spray nozzle, to make their skin look flawless and blemish-free – you do not want to suffer too much by comparison. Men should also try to get a close shave – 5 o'clock shadow looks more noticeable under the lights. Bring in a battery shaver to work, or even a wet-shaving kit, and make sure you look smart before you leave. Television likes 'neat', so check at the last minute that your hair is as tidy-looking as possible. All this is particularly important in an era of high-definition television.

What do you wear for a television interview? For men, it is relatively straightforward. Wear "normal business attire" if you are representing your company, except in special circumstances such as a location interview on an oil rig or food-processing facility, or on a trading floor where you might be perched on the edge of a desk with your sleeves rolled up. It could be a suit or a jacket, with or without tie, according to what feels comfortable and the way you normally dress. As far as shirt colour is concerned, plain shades work best. Try to avoid shirts or jackets with tight stripes or an intricate pattern, as these can sometimes flicker on-screen. Also avoid a dazzlingly white shirt, particularly with a dark suit. On camera, black tends to look blacker than black, and white looks whiter than white; the contrast is too great for the camera, which cannot portray the visual range in the same way as the human eye, so you lose detail and people often end up looking bleached out.

For women it can be a little harder; people do tend to notice what women are wearing to a greater degree. To make life easy for yourself, wear a jacket; this will mean that there will be something that a microphone can be attached to, with the wire hidden behind. If you wear a dress it is harder to hide the microphone cable. Avoid the black/white combo as just described; also bear in mind that plain and clean lines tend to come over better than fiddly patterns. Leave any clunky rings or beads at home in case they clatter on the desk or interfere with the microphone. The key, however, is to dress in an outfit that you feel will make you look good and is appropriate for the circumstances – this in itself will give you confidence. The camera likes neat, clean lines and that applies both to your clothes and to the way you wear your hair. A fuzzy or flyaway look is unflattering. As subtleties can be lost on camera, if you wear a natural-look lipstick it will look on camera as though you are not wearing any lipstick at all. If you wear quite a strong lipstick, such as a bright red or a bright pink, the shade will come across as slightly more muted than in the flesh. Lipstick does lift the look, giving your face more energy and vibrancy.

If you are someone who normally wears glasses, it might be better to take them off if you can possibly do without them for a television interview, but only if you feel comfortable doing so. Particularly if they are thick-rimmed they can act as a barrier between you and the audience, and on occasions can reflect studio lighting. If you feel you need to wear your glasses then you should probably stick with them, but if you are happy either way, or can wear contact lenses, I would recommend this. Certainly do not wear glasses with photo-chromatic lenses that get darker as the light levels increase.

It's almost time...

It should go without saying that if you are going to a live radio or television studio, give yourself plenty of time to get there, making allowances for bad traffic or parking problems. The last thing you want is to arrive breathless and sweaty just as you are due on air

– or even worse, miss the slot. You want to get there in good time, allowing a few moments to check if there have been any last-minute changes to the item or any additional question areas that may not have arisen earlier. Do not expect producers or interviewers to give you much time at this point, as they will be busy – it is a good moment to check hair and makeup for television, and then sit quietly with a coffee. Take several long, slow, deep breaths to relax yourself and focus on what you want to get across once you go live.

If it helps, you can 'psych' yourself up a little, to build confidence – remember, it is a performance. This is the moment to remind yourself of the fact that on radio and television you need to put in lots of energy and project your voice more than you would in an ordinary conversation. If you sound a bit flat and not too enthusiastic about your topic, why would you expect viewers or listeners to care? You have to be a bit larger than life to come over well.

The studio itself can be scary for those who are not familiar with them – you may get that '*this is it*' feeling. A radio studio may be quite small and cramped. Just sit where you are put, and if they ask you to speak a few words into the microphone for sound level, try to give them a few sentences at the same level of voice as you will use once the interview starts. You may be offered headphones, through which the station's output will be played, but you do not need to put these on unless there are participants from another location, such as on a phone-in or call-in show. Some people do find it off-putting to hear their own words blasting at loud volume through the headphones once they start speaking, so it is probably best not to use them unless you need to.

A television studio may be rather larger, with big banks of lights, and sometimes with remotely controlled cameras that can move of their own accord. Do not be intimidated; just make sure you avoid tripping over if there are cables snaking across the floor. The key is to ignore the paraphernalia, and any activity not directly related to you – do not let them put you off. Focus on the job you are there to do. Usually a floor manager will clip a microphone on to you; try very hard not to get too animated during the interview and touch the microphone, as this can sound much louder to the viewer at home than you may realise. You should have put your list of key points away by this stage, as you will look very odd if you keep having to look down to your notes to remind you how to answer a question, You should know what you want to say by now! Ensure your phone is turned off, or at least on 'flight' mode; not just on 'silent' as this can still cause electrical interference.

If you are in the studio you cannot do much about the setting, but if the interview is on location, check the background that will appear in the shot behind you to ensure it looks appropriate – you may want to consider if a company logo could or should be visible, and certainly that there is nothing (or nobody) that would detract from the image you are trying to create. Think how an interview in a food-processing facility would look with someone standing in the background coughing or rubbing their nose.

The last thing is that at this point, even if the interview is live, you will often have a few moments to speak to the interviewer before you begin, perhaps while commercials are playing or a pre-recorded item is broadcast – with live broadcasting this is likely to be the first time you have met. Use this vital time wisely. If you get the chance, build up as much of a relationship as it is possible to do in the space of thirty seconds, or a couple of minutes. The host will rarely want to rehearse elements of the interview, as usually the aim is for you to be 'fresh'. But you can try asking the interviewer how they want to play it, and in particular how they want to kick off the interview – this can buy you vital thinking time, to enable you to get off to a good start. This is important, because if you start well it will help build your confidence, and viewers and listeners are likely to stay tuned – whereas if you start nervously, the audience are likely to switch off and you may find it hard to recover your confidence. If you do feel you have misfired a little, do not look back – take a deep breath during the next question and really give it your all from then on.

Key Reminders

■ *There are far more broadcast opportunities nowadays with a multiplicity of channels and online video material; take what opportunities you can to build your level of experience. Ensure you have had the right training to develop your on-camera skills.*

■ *Find out as much as you can before any broadcast interview, about the style, audience and angle, as well as the practicalities – How long will it be? Will it be live or pre-recorded?*

■ *Make good use of your pre-interview chat with the producer or interviewer to understand as far as possible what points they want to bring out, and suggest angles you think would be helpful.*

■ *Think carefully about what to wear for a television interview in order to create the right image – be aware of what is likely to look good on camera. Television likes neat. Makeup will make you look better on-screen.*

■ *Rehearse your key points so they trip off your tongue – you do not want to be hunting for the right words in the interview itself.*

■ *Do not let yourself be intimidated by your surroundings in a television or radio studio. Ignore the paraphernalia and focus on the job you are there to do.*

■ *If you get the chance, use the couple of minutes before the interview begins to find out how your questioner wants to kick off – this can boost confidence by giving you some extra thinking time, enabling you to create that all-important good first impression.*

Chapter 9

Being great on television and radio

Be clear what you want to get across in the interview

Being great on television and radio

Once you have sorted out any hair and makeup issues, and found out so far as you can how the conversation is likely to be structured, what should you be focusing on during the interview itself? For the inexperienced, it is often simply a matter of survival – their objective is to get through to the end of the interview without drying up or saying anything too disastrous. This of course is a good start, but you can go beyond this. Remember your objectives and what you want to get across, so your subconscious is looking for opportunities during the conversation to get these in. Take a few deep breaths to relax yourself before you start, and try to hit the ground running with lots of energy and verve in that first answer. In chapter 5 I talked about putting together your strongest soundbites, anecdotes and quotes – this is the time to use them.

The television interview

You want the whole impression you create to be consistent, or 'congruent' – in other words for the way you look, your body language, the way you sound, and the message you put across, all to fit together so that nothing jars with the audience. If any of these seem wrong, for instance, if you look far too old or young for your position, or you are too scruffy or dressed inappropriately, or if your voice comes over as lacking authority, they will distract attention from the points you are trying to make, and may even fatally undermine them. If you know you have a particular issue, for example with your voice, or lack of 'presence', professional coaching from an expert can make a big difference – but this is something you would need to think about well in advance.

Either in the studio or on location, the rules on delivery and body language are the same – open and relaxed if possible. Get yourself comfortable once you are in position and ready for the off – you could do your jacket button up if you are standing up and it is an exterior shot on a windy day, to stop the jacket flapping around; otherwise leave it unbuttoned. When sitting down, try not to slump or sit at an angle. Remember that to the viewer you will be framed by the screen, so it is better to look engaged and professional by sitting up alert and straight, with your chest out and your bottom back. Then just relax a little to loosen yourself up and settle the nerves. Some people advise leaning slightly forward. Except in the severest of circumstances, smile – you want to engage with the viewer and create a friendly, open impression. I am not talking about a cheesy over-the-top smile here, more a pleasant twinkle in the eye. Often people are frowning with concentration at this stage and look much more miserable and cheerless than they mean to. This will not convince the audience that it will be a good experience to deal with your organisation.

Try not to rush your delivery. A lot of people don't realise how quickly they are talking, and gabble, particularly when they're nervous. Then, it becomes hard for the viewer to follow. Make that extra bit of effort to make your diction clear, particularly if you have a strong accent of some sort.

Many people find it difficult to know what to do with their hands in a television interview – some people tend to 'talk with their hands'. A degree of movement, for instance to emphasise a point, is fine – but don't let it become distracting. Lots of waving your arms around, with clasped fingers and so on, betray your nerves and will make a television audience nervous, too. If you are sitting behind a desk on set, you can keep any nervously clenched fingers out of sight, otherwise just try to sit still – relax the shoulders and reserve your energy for your vocal delivery. Whatever you do, don't play around with a pen or continually twiddle your fingers if they may be in shot.

The live interview

If circumstances allow, kick off with your strongest point – you are then setting the agenda and can reiterate the point later if you get the chance. Otherwise, there is a danger you will go right off-topic and may not get the point in at all if the right question does not come up. As each question comes, deal with it appropriately; do not duck it even if it is a tricky issue – if relevant you should have expected it to appear during the interview (see chapter 7 on techniques for dealing with difficult questions). Put the matter into context if necessary. Look out for anything that would allow you legitimately to inject one of your key points or 'extras'.

Keep your eye-line to the interviewer, as you want to look focused, not shifty. This is really key to the impression you create. Many people look up or down when they are trying to think about what they want to say. However, if you do not appear to be looking the interviewer in the eye, you arouse suspicion that you are not telling the truth – body language experts can read quite a lot into exactly how you react when you are answering a question truthfully, as opposed to when you may be trying to hide something. The simple rule to remember is just to keep that eye-line focused. If, as sometimes happens in a studio debate, you are asked questions by more than one person, deliver your answer to the person who asked the question, so any eye-line movement will tend to occur while you are listening, rather than while you are speaking. With a down-the-line interview, you will hear the questions through an earpiece or small loudspeaker – in these circumstances you have to look directly into the camera, treating it as if it were a person. Many people find this awkward at first, so they really benefit from practice during a television media training session. Try not to be self-conscious; chat into the camera as normally as you can – it will probably look better to the viewer than it feels to you at the time. For more on talking direct to camera if you are creating your own video content, see chapter 10.

From then on it is mainly a matter of consistency – try to keep up the generally warm impression, keep up the energy level, keep the eye-line steady, and keep the focus on what you want to get across. If you are unlucky enough to get a question that is off-topic for you in a broadcast interview (it may be that a producer or interviewer has agreed not to ask about a particular issue, but then goes ahead and asks anyway), you cannot say, as you might have done during a non-broadcast interview, "That's not really an issue that I'm involved in; you'd better speak to our media relations person and they can help you more than I can" – you would sound silly. Instead, try to move on without drawing attention to it. You could perhaps say something like, "Well that's not an area I am involved in, but the point I would make is..." or, "I'm not really the person to ask about that – it's a matter for the remuneration committee – but it's certainly not an issue that's affecting us. In fact..." If the interviewer is persistent, this is not the time to change your tune. Keep your cool, and so long as you have got a tenable position, stick to it.

Gladiatorial interviews

Of course, if you are giving a responsibility interview (ie where you are answerable for your organisation's activities; see chapter 2) and your position is not tenable under scrutiny, you should either have prepared a better answer, or not have agreed to do the interview at all. If you keep adding to the information you give every time an interviewer pushes, all you are doing is motivating him or her to carry on pushing, because it obviously gets results. On occasion, an interview that begins in a relatively straightforward way can suddenly turn into something very different. This tends to be a phenomenon of the political interview – politicians are viewed by the media in most countries as responsible to the electorate, and as highly practised and proficient interviewees, often given to incorporating great degrees of 'spin' into their answers – and therefore fair game if there are difficult issues to be addressed.

Some of the most famous 'gladiatorial' interviews on British television have come when the interrogator persists with a line of questioning if the answers appear to be evasive, putting the interviewee under increasing levels of pressure. A famous example was the 1997 BBC *Newsnight* interview with Conservative politician Michael Howard, where interviewer Jeremy Paxman asked the same question twelve times. Part of the reason such occasions stick in the memory is that confrontations like this are in fact very rare, even for politicians. It is even more unusual for members of the public and business representatives to be given such a ferocious grilling, although of course not unprecedented in particular circumstances, – for example, bankers who were perceived as culpable during the banking crisis, or the then BP chief executive Tony Hayward in the wake of the Deepwater Horizon oil spillage. Any executive caught in this type of crisis would have the full panoply of PR and crisis management support, and should practise, practise, practise before going on the air.

Fortunately, to repeat, these circumstances are very unusual. In fact, there are hundreds of hours of interviews on British radio and television every week, and the vast majority are about 'information' rather than 'confrontation' – the same applies to other countries. That does not mean that there will not be difficult questions other than in a crisis – of course there will. The aim is not usually just to give you a free piece of PR, but rather to create an entertaining or probing conversation that gives some sort of balance between the positives and the drawbacks of the topic. It should come over as broadly fair-minded. Sometimes interviewers get that balance right; sometimes they do not. In fact, I have seen many cases where the interviewer has been too tough, leading to the audience's sympathy being for the interviewee.

Typically, it is a matter of style – interviewers want to be seen as having put the right questions to their subjects, not just letting them off the hook if there are contentious issues to be discussed – so if you give a good answer everyone is happy. Interviewers are often just playing devil's advocate to ensure the arguments are properly tested. Do not necessarily mistake this for hostility, although it can feel like this at the time – they are simply doing their job, by putting the questions on behalf of their audience. You have to do your job by having a good answer ready.

Try not to let yourself be put off by persistent questioning. Keep your cool, and answer the questions. If they do keep coming back, then restate your main points calmly and clearly and say something like, "As I've said, there's not a lot more I can add to that, for the reason…" Keep smiling, whatever the provocation. Do not allow yourself to get angry, because the audience will see you are rattled. If you are calm and the interviewer gets angry with you, that becomes their problem, and you may well be the one who comes off better. Whatever you do, never walk out on an interview, however much the provocation;, because that can in itself become the story.

Soundbite interviews

So much for the live interview, but what about the pre-recorded interview when the broadcaster is just looking for a nice, punchy soundbite – maybe the ten or twenty seconds that is the pithy quote that really sums up your argument. This can become a building block for a short news report, or a long-form current affairs show or documentary. Interviewers, if they are doing their jobs properly, will be trained to ask open questions, the sort of 'who, what, why, where' types of questions that require broad answers rather than just a yes or no response. You have to bear this in mind when you reply. Reporters want a self-explanatory answer, one that does not require the viewer to have heard the question in order to be able to understand the response. If the interview runs along the following lines, the reporter will have nothing he or she can use:

Q: Will this new tax make a big difference in your ability to compete in difficult markets?

A: *Yes it will.*

Much better would be:

Q: How much will this new tax affect your ability to compete in difficult markets?

A: *This new tax will make it far harder to compete in the current difficult markets, potentially leading to the loss of hundreds of jobs...*

In the second example, the answer incorporates the sense of the question, and makes a powerful statement that stands on its own. This is what you should aim for where possible. Think about trying to wrap the essence of the matter that you are trying to put across in to one punchy point. That requires a bit of thought and a bit of rehearsal – but it will be worth it. Find out beforehand roughly what length of soundbite they are likely to be looking for – although in truth this will be to some extent up to you. If you are delivering good value material to the audience, they will use more of the interview than if you turn out to be rather dull.

Bear in mind that when a reporter is interviewing you for a soundbite they may seem to be asking you the same question over and over again. This could be because they want to elicit the best possible answer from you, or because of a noise in the background, or in a tough interview because they are pushing you to say more than you are able to. Keep your cool and do not be afraid to repeat your key points, but perhaps in a slightly different form, for example by giving them a longer version and a shorter version. This gives them plenty of flexibility and increases the chance they will end up with something usable. More proficient and practised interviewees – those with the M-factor – will weave their key messages into several responses. If you trip over your words, or realise your response is heading in an inappropriate direction, it does not matter. Because the interview is pre-recorded, you can stop in the middle and start again. Reporters are looking for an articulate, concise delivery and it is better for you to try again than for them to have to use something that does not really work. If there is an important piece of context you need to get across, try to weave it into your answers, so it does not simply get cut out.

The radio interview

Everything I have said in terms of content and delivery for television interviews also applies to the radio interview. You need to check what is required, that you are the right person, and ensure you have some clear messages and soundbites ready. You can argue, with some justification, that if you can manage a television interview you can do a radio interview as well. After all, with television you have a lot more to think about – How do you look? Where do you look? Do you have any strange mannerisms that will make you look silly on the air? However, there are some aspects that are particularly worth thinking about if you are invited to give a radio interview.

The first point is that radio can be an 'instant' medium – unlike television, which either requires you to go to the studio or for them to send a crew. With radio, they can call you up and patch you through, putting you on the air within seconds by phone if necessary. Do not allow yourself to be bounced into giving an instant interview if you are not ready. Give yourself a few minutes to jot down and run through your key points. The good news is that, unlike television, you can keep this list in front of you. Glance down every so often during the interview if you want to, as a reminder – very useful if you fear your mind suddenly going blank.

With both radio and television you need to make an effort to sound lively and interested rather than monotonous and boring – an extra 20% of energy above your standard speaking voice is usually about right. You are, after all, in the entertainment business here. On television you need to make sure that this energy does not mean arms flailing about and head bobbing – hugely annoying and distracting for viewers – but on the radio this does not matter. Bob around as much as you want, if this helps you to make your performance lively and engaging – just make sure you do not get too carried away and hit the microphone. Unless it is a really serious or sombre topic, inject some warmth into your voice by lightening up your expression – as they say, you can 'smile on the radio' and listeners will definitely hear it.

Obviously, telephone interviews are a lot more common on the radio than the television. If this opportunity appears and you are at home or in the office, find a quiet room and shut the door behind you – ensure colleagues, small children and noisy pets are kept well away so you do not get distracted. Talk on a landline, as mobile or cellphone signals are weaker and can sometimes drop out. In fact, turn your personal devices off so that they do not go off during the interview. Have a glass of water ready in case your throat becomes dry. Make sure you know your audience and that you pitch what you are saying appropriately – no confusing jargon. Radio is a medium for big-picture general points, not nitpicking detail.

If you are selling something, make very sure you do not over-sell it. There is little that is more annoying to the listener (and the host) than somebody who brazenly and repeatedly takes it too far with product plugs – people will just switch off, and then you have achieved nothing. You might get away with it the first time, but you are unlikely to be invited back; it is much more important to be entertaining than pushy. Try to aim for a lively interplay between you and the presenter.

A mistake people often make is to rush through – it is better to slow down, so that what you say comes over clearly. If you have a strong accent, or are not being interviewed in your native language, it is particularly important not to feel pressured to speak too quickly – otherwise few will understand what you are saying. The listener can only focus on your voice, so try to make it warm, and your style varied and interesting. Some people advise standing up as you talk, as your breathing won't be constrained and your lungs can open fully, so you can really perform.

Finally, unless the subject is sombre, as with any broadcast inter-view, remember to enjoy yourself. If you are having a good time, the interview is likely to be fun to watch or listen to for the audience.

Key Reminders

■ *You want your body language to match your delivery – open and relaxed if possible. Find a comfortable, upright sitting position and try to stick with it – no nervous twitching.*

■ *Eye-line is key with a television interview – either look directly at the interviewer, or into the camera as appropriate – avoid the 'shifty' look of eyes darting about.*

■ *With a live interview it is vital to hit the ground running, otherwise viewers and listeners will not bother to stay tuned. If possible get your key point out right at the start.*

■ *Answer the questions as best you can, but don't slavishly follow the interviewer and forget about the points you actually wanted to make.*

■ *Stay cool and calm, even under pressure from a provocative interviewer. Don't be afraid to repeat what you have said, if it is your best way of dealing with the issue.*

■ *On radio, try to match the style of the show – many are focused more on entertainment value than hard information. All your communication comes through your voice, so be lively.*

■ *If you are giving a telephone interview, find a quiet room where you will not be distracted – with a landline phone unless there is absolutely no other option.*

Chapter 10

Social media and online video

Social media: you can't just leave it to teenagers

FACTOR

Social media and online video

The world of social media is fast-changing and the rules are fluid, but some broad principles seem to be emerging. The first point, that many find it hard to cope with, is that social media are by their very nature two-way rather than one-way. Many large organisations fail to 'get' this, and tend simply to transmit information, rather than also being on 'receive'. Of course, big businesses in particular like to be in control, and this is what they find difficult. As I have said in the context of traditional mass media however, if you do not join the conversation you cannot set the agenda. This may be via text-based opportunities such as blogging, Facebook and Twitter, or video-based, such as a YouTube channel.

All organisations need to consider getting involved in social media, if for no other reason that if they hit reputational difficulties of any sort, they will otherwise be unable to use these vital channels to convey their message; communicate to stakeholders; and put right any misinformation that is being broadcast about them by others. So it is wise to embrace this world as soon as possible - get used to it and its strange ways, so that you know how to deal with it if you have to. Social media can be used to get your own content out into the market, and as an effective means of customer service support; to be viewed as a mainstream communications channel for brand and reputation management. It could be argued that every company, whatever its nominal business sector, is now in the communications business – all brands are now media brands.

This is not the place for tutorials on Twitter, LinkedIn and so on. Most large organisations already have a definite social media strategy; if yours is the exception, you should encourage it to create one if you are in a position to do so, even if you are in a purely business-to-business market. Often the media relations department will be in charge of content and monitoring, and you should take up-to-date advice from the experts on this. Which social channels are appropriate for you will depend on the type of sector you are in; Facebook may be rather less relevant for a components supply business than for a consumer brand aimed at the 18-24 market. Generally speaking, the style and tone of your social media communication should be conversational, rather than formal and corporate; this is certainly not just another route for pumping out your company press releases.

Social media opportunities

Every day, smart companies across the world are coming up with new ways to sell more product via social media, by engaging with their customers. In many ways what they are having to do is create their own content, much like a magazine, newspaper or television channel would. Often a journalistic approach is appropriate here – it is about thinking what the audience is interested in, then giving it useful and relevant material. However, smart use of social media is increasingly valuable when dealing with traditional, mass media outlets.

To take one example, some journalists now use Twitter to make contact with people who may have interesting views on a topic they are writing or broadcasting about. For instance, the BBC's Technology correspondent has on occasion, in the wake of specific news events, appealed for analysts who can comment about the developments to come forward for possible interview. This way he can reach people anywhere in the world, with whom he is otherwise unlikely to have connected, to give an alternative perspective to the 'experts' he already knows. The connection may occur with someone who is already following him on Twitter, because he frequently tweets useful news updates and snippets. Or, it may be because he uses the 'hashtag' of a trending topic of the day, and those following this particular topic find his message that way. Or, he spots an interesting comment on Twitter, and makes direct contact with the individual concerned to follow up. This is a great way for those trying to raise their profile to make the 'breakthrough' into mass media. Look out for relevant correspondents who are active on social media, to see what they are saying and what they are interested in. What can you learn or what can you comment on to get yourself noticed? In the US there is a website called Help A Reporter Out, which exists purely to put journalists in touch with people who might have interesting things to say. Gorkana in the UK does something similar.

Blogs provide another opportunity. If you have a company or personal blog which is followed only by a few die-hard fans, your influence is likely to be limited. However, if you research the most widely-followed blogs in your sector and start following them, you may see comment opportunities, which can link through to your own blog. For easy monitoring you can use a service such as Google Reader, which you can use to aggregate all the blogs you are following in the one place, and to see how popular they are. If you are interesting enough for your comments to be picked up by one of these super-bloggers, you may suddenly have a worldwide audience, and attract the attention of traditional media. Some sectors, such as the tech sector, have particularly influential online commentators who are very widely followed, and are now treated by PR firms like mainstream journalists, with access to advance information and gadgets for review. Other aggregation, blogging and social media sites ranging from Huffington Post and Mashable to Mumsnet have created new ways to reach various target audiences.

Social media threats

You need to have the right monitoring in place, so you know if there are conversations going on about you behind your back, to which you can swiftly respond if necessary. Twitter is particularly important here, because it is currently the easiest way for a single customer complaint about you to gain widespread traction, or even go global, through re-tweeting. However there are others, such as Facebook groups, which have been used to get disaffected customers to band together and make a big noise about some piece of real or imagined corporate misbehaviour; banks and other large corporates have been targeted. On occasion, company Facebook pages have been turned against their creators. For instance in 2012 the feminine hygiene brand Femfresh ran a light-hearted UK advertising campaign across a variety of media, jokily referring to a string of slang words for female genitalia. This campaign was perceived as be condescending and sexist by many women and some men, who posted a huge number of negative comments on Femfresh's own Facebook page, turning the page into a platform for protest, rather than a promotional tool. The company was slow to respond, then attracted further opprobrium by deleting some of the comments, instead of engaging with the debate. It also led to wider protests about the product itself, which would otherwise not have been given an audience. Eventually the company had to suspend its Facebook account altogether. An open and honest apology would have been a better response; or a creative approach to harness the contributions, many of which were witty, to get its followers back on-side.

To keep as far ahead as you can, the key is to identify the issues that matter and the people that matter – for instance certain Premier League footballers have over 1.5 million Twitter followers at the time of writing, making them in social media terms far more important than their team-mates. Who are the big influencers in your area? Ensure you are following them, and respond quickly and with great care if need be.

An increase in complaint levels, or a specific incident where your customer care is perceived to have fallen short, can very suddenly 'go viral' and escalate into something far more significant. Your aim should be to nip such problems in the bud, before they spiral out of control. The impact can be particularly noticeable when social media and 'traditional media' interact and feed off each other. So, some negative tweets about your business may be picked up and re-tweeted by influential individuals with thousands of followers. These in turn are monitored by local, trade or national newspaper journalists on the lookout for material. One of them takes notice, and follows up. The story is uploaded to the publication's website, and its journalists tweet the link to their own followers, cranking up the outrage factor a few notches. Other publications pick up the story, more members of the public tweet their "me too" stories - leading to the perception that the original 'victims' were far from an isolated example of your poor customer treatment, however fair or unfair that perception may be. You have a crisis on your hands. For more on crisis handling see Chapter 11.

There is no 'correct' way to handle a social media crisis; each situation can evolve in different, unpredictable ways, depending on how much traction it gains. Luck can certainly come into it. All being well, your media team or PR advisers will be experienced enough to make the best judgement as to when to get involved and when to stand back. It may feel like you cannot win – if you reply to critical tweets from your company's twitter account, that in itself can draw more attention to the problem, but if you do not engage, then that can be judged as being even worse. Usually, the best course of action is to ensure you have an effective complaints handling system in place, and contact anyone making serious criticisms personally to see if they can be resolved as early as possible. Listen to see if it is a one-off problem, or if there is something bigger happening – if so, fix it. One of the downsides of social media is that they can encourage a self-righteous mob mentality. Once people see a group opinion gain traction, they often find it hard not to join in and share the outrage.

If you are a big brand with a lot of public interest, you do not necessarily have to answer all customer questions individually – many can be dealt with by responding to enquirers swiftly, pointing them to a Frequently Asked Questions area. Many larger companies how have a specific channel or forum for customer service, so they can demonstrate socially that when problems do arise, they are dealt with properly. This helps keep such issues away from the main company Twitter account or Facebook page – at least in normal circumstances.

Try not to panic if someone is slinging mud, as sometimes complainants are just trying it on; the whole thing may fizzle out. If things have moved beyond this stage, use your Twitter feed to justify your actions if appropriate, and show what action you are taking to remedy the situation, emphasising positive company policies. Acknowledge and apologise if you get something wrong. Be respectful in your tone, even if others are intemperate; reinforce your corporate values. Use the right hashtags so everyone can see you have engaged and responded. Monitor news alerts to check on media follow-up, and ensure you are in direct contact with any journalists who have shown an interest in the issue. It is unrealistic to expect you to be able to use Twitter to convey your messages in under 140 characters, but you can use Twitter to alert the media to any announcements or link to news updates on your website, as with the River Cottage fire in our case study on page 139. If possible, have your own compelling narrative that you can get across forcefully – for example "we adhere to the highest safety standards in the industry" .. or "our guiding principle is to ..." Each communication in a crisis should reinforce this.

Think what your social media guidelines for staff should be in a crisis – if you allow them to comment freely, you have no idea what they may put out, so some guidance is probably in order. However if you appear too over-controlling that can count against you; this is a very sensitive issue in the social media world. As an example of this, though not involving staff, in 2012 Argyll and Bute Council became increasingly defensive about criticisms of the lunches provided at one of its schools, from a single schoolgirl, Martha Payne, who set up a blog called NeverSeconds. Here, she posted pictures of what she had been given to eat each day, which looked relatively unappealing. The council's attempts to silence her attracted widespread ridicule, and led to a massive boost to the number of hits on the girl's blog, which ran to over two million. The council eventually had to reverse its decision.

As ever, speed is of the essence. Your organisation should be mobile-enabled for social media so that if necessary, responses can easily be given around the clock. Have an agreed approval process in place so you can get messages out speedily – a committee-based approval system does not work for social media, especially in a crisis. For instance, after the BlackBerry phone maker RIM had a well-publicised system outage in the UK in 2011, users in a number of countries were unable to receive their e-mails over two days, or use the BBM messaging system. The company was extremely slow to explain to angry users via their website and social media what was going on; it then eventually tweeted in highly technical, non user-friendly language, which grated even more. In the meantime,

BlackBerry users around the world vented their frustration via a variety of social media platforms, which contributed to the company's fast-declining reputation. If RIM had been more open and transparent, customers would of course still have been frustrated at the loss of service, but brand reputation would have suffered less long-term damage as the situation was resolved.

Case Study

LA Fitness

Gym chain LA Fitness faced negative publicity in the UK early in 2012, over highly restrictive membership contracts from which people were apparently unable to extricate themselves, even when their circumstances changed dramatically. This culminated in a story in The Guardian about a couple who were being held to a two-year contract they could not afford, even when she became pregnant, he lost his job and they were about to move away from the gym catchment area. A storm of negative Twitter publicity followed, which the company seemed unable to counter effectively, initially saying "we do not comment on individual cases" before changing its mind and backing down. By this time lots of people had vowed never to pay money to the chain again. The fact the 'Twitterstorm' had occurred was followed up, and had almost become the story itself.

In cases like this, companies should try to use their Twitter presence more positively, correcting any inaccuracies in news articles, and putting their side of the story. In fact, well before crisis strikes. many consumer-facing companies could do much more to build up a following by giving special offers, deals, competitions and so on to build a community and goodwill. Then, they have built up their own 'tribe', and have a direct conduit to those people, ready to use if needed if they are being criticised.

Case Study

River Cottage Restaurant

In February 2012 a fire burnt down the 17th Century River Cottage Barn at Axminster in Devon, part of the restaurant and cookery school business run by food writer and celebrity chef Hugh Fearnley-Whittingstall. Eighty firefighters were called out to tackle the blaze. No-one was hurt, but courses and events had to be cancelled and the event attracted widespread attention because of River Cottage's television profile. Telephone lines at the site were down so social media were used as a key means of communicating to customers and the media. In particular, Twitter became the communication channel the company used to 'develop key messages, share updates and inform audiences'. A feed of information was transmitted, including links to updates and photos and videos posted on the River Cottage website and Facebook, as well as plenty of re-tweeting of supportive messages from customers and answers to customer questions, thanking them for their messages of goodwill. It all contributed to a feeling of shared experience with River Cottage customers.

The fire and its aftermath attracted interest from local and national media, which relied on these social media channels for updates, enabling River Cottage to remain in control of the story. Customers were reassured and given information on bookings, and when the facilities would re-open; within a couple of weeks it was back to 'business as usual' in a temporary facility. Social media had helped get updates and information out quickly and accurately, and provided a factual resource for journalists, as well as becoming a place for positive support and feedback from the public. River Cottage generated goodwill and good press over its quick

Continued/...

recovery from the incident. The outcome was an increase in customer engagement and follower numbers, a reduced short-term impact on the business and maintained reputation. The company says the lessons are to act quickly, say what you will do and do it, provide Twitter links to images and video for content, and ask followers to spread the word.

Online Video

Increasingly, both small and large companies see online video as an important part of their communications armoury, whether on their own website, or in social terms, such as a YouTube channel. What is appropriate here very much depends on whether your market is consumer or business, and how you are positioned. It is clear, however, that the ability to communicate effectively on video is increasingly important in business, whether directly on a website, or through webcasts, webinars, internal communications, video inserts to conference presentations – the list goes on. When in the eye of a storm, such as a damaging strike, companies such as British Airways and Eurostar have used YouTube to communicate directly to customers, bypassing the traditional media gatekeepers; we will see more of this. Any ambitious manager should now make it his or her business to be able to talk comfortably to camera.

If the video takes the form of an interview, the same rules apply as with broadcast TV in terms of eye-line – see Chapter 9. However a lot of the time you may have to talk direct to camera, which is something a lot of people find awkward. So what can you do to increase your chances of looking cool, calm, collected and professional?

Ten techniques to help you talk easily to camera

1   Get in the right frame of mind

A lot of people get nervous as soon as the camera is switched on; they get sweaty, look shifty and their voice becomes cracked. Have a sip of water to hand, and calm any nerves beforehand with some deep breathing exercises. The camera may be quite close up on you, so every smile or facial tic will be visible. Give yourself a few moments to focus and get into the right frame of mind, and practise your smile to create a good first impression.

2   Sit comfortably

Sit up straight, then relax a little so you do not look too stiff. Ideally try to arrange things so that the camera is at eye level, rather than looking down at you, or - even worse – looking up your nose. Try to keep your chin at a neutral level, rather than jutting forward or tightening up your throat and constricting your vocal chords. Shoulders should be relaxed and balanced, not hunched or tensed.

3   Don't jiggle

Small movements can be exaggerated on camera in close-up, so try not to jiggle about. Try practising beforehand in front of the mirror, talking in a lively, animated way but without moving your head around too much – you want to put the energy in your voice instead. If you are someone who 'talks with their hands', try to ensure they do not fly in and out of shot. Establish how much of you will be in shot, and try and keep hand movements below that.

4   **The eyes have it**

*When you look into the camera, try to think of the lens
as a person you are chatting to. The cold, unblinking eye
of the camera can be very off-putting, as it gives you no
visual feedback like a person would. Sometimes people
even stick a snap of a family member just above the lens,
and imagine they are talking to that individual. Otherwise
try to look directly into the lens, rather than just below
it. Do not 'mirror' the camera's lack of recognition by
staring at it, glassy-eyed and unblinking; the 'rabbit-in-
the-headlights' look. Instead you should consciously blink
a little more often than you usually would – avoiding the
other extreme of blinking too often, as this will signal your
discomfort. Try as hard as hard as you can to keep looking
straight into the camera; if your eyes flicker around, either
from left to right or up and down, you will appear shifty to
your audience.*

5   **Smile!**

*See if you can convey warmth in your eyes rather than
externalise your anxiety.   I usually find people are
concentrating so hard when they do anything in front of
camera, that they look much more serious, grumpy, or
plain petrified, than they realise. So, avoid a cheesy grin
that you awkwardly put on only when you remember,
but try and consciously put a bit of a smile on your face.
Establish this two or three seconds before you begin your
performance, so your audience does not see you switch
from frown to smile. Then keep it there as you work
through your material.*

6 Be chatty

Put plenty of energy in, and use a friendly, conversational tone rather than a formal one. You are talking to people rather than at them; unlike a presentation in front of a room full of people, your audience will usually be made up of single individuals. You want each of them to think you are communicating with them personally, so avoid referring to them in the plural, for instance by saying "all of you".

7 Extemporise if you can ...

If possible resist the temptation to read from a script, unless you have a lot of material to get through; even with an autocue/teleprompter system set up, many people, without training, find it very hard to breathe life into a script, and can sound wooden. For a shorter piece, try and memorise what you want to say, in sections if necessary which can be stitched together using editing shots. For longer, more informal pieces, for instance a webinar, you could print out your key bullet points in big typeface, on a piece of paper which you can stick or prop up immediately above or below the camera lens, as a reminder to keep you on track. Try not to let your eyes flicker around though. Again, looking directly into the lens is always preferable if you can manage it, compared with looking slightly below it; however as long as you are not too close-up in shot most viewers will not notice the slight shift in eye-line. If you do have to briefly look down to the desk between points to check your notes, make it look deliberate and planned, not a furtive glance. Blink as you do so, so your audience is less likely to notice your eyes darting about.

8   ... Otherwise bring your script to life

If you have a lot of material to get through and want to read from a script, it is best to have an autocue or teleprompt system set up. A professional system uses a mirror in front of the camera which enables you to read your words scrolling in front of you, while still making direct eye contact with the viewer; an operator will vary the speed the text moves to match your reading speed. However if budget does not allow, there are now low-cost or free alternatives which, with a bit of effort, can achieve almost the same effect for short blocks of script. For example basic teleprompter kits are now available which use an iPad to provide the scrolling text while you look into the camera lens; however it can take a lot of practice to get the scrollling speed just right. Or, more simply still, you can set your text scrolling lengthways across a smartphone screen with a clever app such as PromptWare Plus; again you will have to experiment with the scrolling speed to match your particular delivery style. Position your phone immediately above the camera lens with tape or Blu-tack, and with a bit of practice few people will notice the difference. Either way, go through the script out loud beforehand, changing any words that do not sound natural, and write it in conversational not formal written language – for example use 'don't' rather than 'do not' which usually sounds awkward when spoken. Make sure you vary your tone to make your delivery sound more interesting, and think which words you should emphasise to make the meaning as clear as possible.

9   No need to rush

Something happens to a lot of people when they are nervous – they start gabbling and have no idea how quickly they are speaking. Then they wonder why they tie themselves up in verbal knots and come to a dead halt – because their brain cannot keep up with their lips. Take it easy, you are probably going faster than you realise. Pause for two to three seconds between points, to give them time to sink in with the audience, and for you to gather your thoughts for the next point you want to make.

10   Don't wing it!

You want to sound as professional as possible if representing your organisation. If you continually fluff your lines, this will add to the pressure when recording, and you will fluff your lines more. Run through your material properly beforehand so you feel very familiar with it. If you are doing a live webcast and make mistakes however, try not to let this put you off. Do not draw attention to your errors – clarify what you are trying to say, take a deep breath before your next point, then keep going with a smile not a frown on your face, looking forwards not back.

Key Reminders

■ *No organisation can afford to ignore social media nowadays. Establish a social media presence so you can monitor what is being said about you, and communicate to customers and other stakeholders.*

■ *The social media 'rules' are likely to continue to evolve. Anything deemed 'inappropriate' behaviour by companies can generate a fierce online backlash.*

■ *Language should be more conversational than corporate. Think of a conversation as opposed to just a transmission mechanism for company messages.*

■ *In a crisis use social media to correct any misinformation about the situation, answer questions, and keep customers and the media informed about what steps you are taking to resolve things.*

■ *Speed is of the essence in handling criticism.*

■ *Online video is playing an increasingly important role in corporate communication. It is smart to ensure you acquire the skills to create a good impression on camera, rather than looking unprofessional.*

■ *When addressing the camera, try not to let your eyes wander. Memorise short sections if you can, rather than trying to read from a script. For longer pieces, use an autocue/teleprompt system.*

Chapter 11

Six golden rules for dealing with a media crisis

In the wake of a crisis you have to show your humanity

FACTOR

Six golden rules for dealing with a media crisis

What do we mean by a 'crisis'? As I have discovered from dealing with a variety of organisations, one man's crisis is another man's, "It's not been too bad a day really." In this chapter I am thinking of something that goes beyond a bit of bad PR, and becomes something that could dramatically affect the organisation if badly handled. There is a whole industry focused on crisis and reputation management, and it is beyond the scope of this book to go into exhaustive detail. However, if you or someone in the organisation has not already done so, you need to work with your management team and PR colleagues to ensure you are ready for action in these six key areas. If you do this, you will be better prepared than most.

1. Integrate media into your business continuity planning

Big companies have whole departments devoted to business continuity planning, and they should at least have done the bare minimum to ensure the business can continue to operate should it be hit by explosion or fire at the datacentre, occupation by political activists, mass food poisoning in the canteen or malfunctioning of the products on the shelves – or whatever the potential threat is perceived to be. These are the basic life support functions of the company. But often the greatest threat is reputational – if you are seen to have been incompetent in handling events then that can do more long-term damage than the financial cost of putting right the 'crisis' in the first place.

Yet I suspect many company crisis plans are very thin on how they would handle the media aspect, or make woefully inadequate assumptions about the level of media interest. One European insurance company, which shall remain nameless, is said to have assumed that in the event of its large headquarters building being incapacitated or attacked, the media would be held in a separate building a quarter of a mile away and would put up with being drip-fed information. This is laughable. Another used the working assumption that reporters would not be allowed on to its property in the event of a crisis, so the company would be able to control access, filming and so on. When the worst happened, nobody remembered to tell the security guards, who in the confusion just said, "You'd better come in," when the television crews rolled up. Once on site, they were impossible to remove without causing an almighty rumpus that would have led to even further negative publicity. Much 'headless chicken' footage appeared on screen.

You should ensure that the practicalities of media handling have been fully incorporated in your plans, proportionate to the level of media interest that is likely to be generated. For a large multinational with a well-known brand name, this will clearly be greater than for a smaller local company. Even in the latter case, however, it can be a lot more than you think. Once the crisis hits, it is far too late to sit down and plan; instead, that is the time to put your plans into action. Well beforehand, you should think about whether reporters and television crews are likely to turn up at your premises if you have a problem. If so, who would handle interviews, as well as the flood of other media calls that might ensue? Who would decide how much information would be provided, and when? Have you got enough media-trained spokespeople, with backups in case the first choice is away or unavailable? How would you handle media enquiries if your main switchboard is down? Would you impose strict rules on use of social media by staff, or would you allow people to tweet what they like? What messages would you be wanting to communicate in a crisis to customers, suppliers, regulators and shareholders? Do you have a blank page ready to bring to life on the corporate website with up-to-date information in the event of a problem, or a dedicated 'dark site'? Do you have battery backup for phones, laptops and radios (to find out what is going on) in the event of a major incident with no power to the HQ building? Who would handle internal communications and brief receptionists and security guards as to how they should deal with enquiries?

2. Establish potential threats

Of course, you can never predict every possible threat – indeed you would probably drive yourself mad trying to do so. However, you should be able to work out the most likely categories of potential threat, with some base-line responses for each, which can be used as starting points if something occurs. For each of your key stakeholders (customers, staff, suppliers, etc.) you should plan your basic message, and means of communicating it. Depending on your business, the categories of potential threat might include:

- *large-scale breakdown of service caused by external or internal factors, eg fire, flood, software malfunction*

- *death or injury to customers that could be blamed on the company's products or services, eg food poisoning in a hotel chain or restaurant, coach crash for a travel company*

- *financial loss to business or customers due to fraud or data theft by staff or 'rogue trader'*

- *high-profile campaign launched against business by activists, eg on environmental, animal rights, tax avoidance issues*

- *deliberate attack on business, eg cyber-attack, food- or medicine-tampering*

- *reputational damage through sustained/unexpected stakeholder criticism, eg shareholder activists, health service patients groups, trade unions.*

Possible standard messages you might want to be ready to use, or build on, could include:

- *"We are working closely with the emergency services and other relevant authorities and we appreciate the job they are doing. We will continue to fully co-operate with them."*

- *"Our people are working incredibly hard to resolve this and I want to thank them."*

- *"We are shocked at what has happened and want to extend our sympathy to the families of those involved."*

- *"In more than thirty years in business, this is the first time we have been affected in this way."*

- *"We pride ourselves in our professional approach. We will be launching a full investigation into what has happened and will do everything in our power to ensure it can never happen again."*

- *"We strongly condemn this action, which we believe to be completely unjustified, because..."*

3. Understand the importance of quick response

It may sound banal to say so, but in a crisis time really is of the essence. This particularly applies to any major crisis that arises from a sudden, unexpected event such as fire or flood. In these circumstances, think of what is known as the 'golden hour' immediately afterwards.

What you do then as an organisation is likely to set the tone from there on, and it is incredibly hard to recover if you get it wrong at this stage. Fairly or unfairly, the media get a sense almost at once where you fall on the following scales:

competent	**incompetent**
unlucky victims	**to blame**
worth talking to	**not worth talking to**
in control of events	**at the mercy of events**
open, transparent organisation	**closed, controlling organisation**
organised	**'headless chickens'**

In the aftermath of a large-scale incident, the tone will usually be set by the television news channels; all major news organisations monitor their coverage. 'Citizen journalists' may send in pictures before the professionals get there, and mobile phone video footage. Social media news sources such as Twitter are now very influential in some cases; the first reports of events as diverse as the 2009 near-disaster when a US Airways pilot was forced to bring his plane down in the Hudson river, and the military attack on Osama bin Laden's compound in Pakistan, came via Twitter almost as soon as they had happened.

Gone are the days, therefore, when the organisation at the heart of an event is liable to be the only major source of news about it. In other words, if you do not give journalists the information they seek, they will go elsewhere. The news channels will fill airtime with speculation if you make no comment, or go to competitors, 'experts', angry customers, bystanders, the emergency services – anyone they can find to speak to. So if you want to set the agenda you should make your organisation the essential source of information the media cannot ignore. The earlier you can make some sort of statement the better.

The temptation is to avoid making any comment in the early stages because you are not in possession of all the facts. I have news for you – by the time you are in possession of all the facts, it will be far, far too late. Think of releasing an early 'holding statement' as soon as possible, confirming the bare facts of what has happened, promising to make further information available as soon as you can. Stick only to known facts, do not speculate – but you can make use of any stock responses as appropriate of the type given in the list above. If there are television cameras, make someone who is well trained available to make these basic points on camera in a calm and responsible way – when under considerable pressure this is not an easy thing to do; I have seen people completely go to pieces when we run crisis media training exercises along these lines. Again, this initial response will set the tone for how you are perceived, so effective training for potential spokespeople is essential.

For a less high-profile event, the sense of urgency may not be quite so intense, and the news cameras may be absent – but the same principle applies. Respond as quickly as possible and take control of events rather than being controlled by them.

Case study: Bernard Matthews

In February 2007, it was discovered that H5N1 (bird flu) had broken out at a Bernard Matthews' turkey farm at Holton in Suffolk. While the true origin of the infection was never conclusively proved, the strand of H5N1 was genetically almost identical to that which had previously caused an outbreak in

Hungary, where the company owned a subsidiary. Bernard Matthews, the UK's largest turkey producer, initially denied a link, saying all its birds were 'home grown'. However, the accidental discovery of a wrapper revealed it had actually been importing some turkeys from Hungary. The company had initially maintained that operations in Hungary and Suffolk were entirely separate with no trade between them, but after several days it admitted that not only was there significant trade between the plants, but that it could have imported infected turkey meat. MPs and consumer groups accused the company of concealing the fact it imported large numbers of poultry and legally labelled them British. While the imports were shown to be from outside Hungary's infected zone, the damage was already done – public trust had fallen sharply. According to BBC reports, sales slumped by about 40% and the company had to lay off a part of its workforce.

The company was criticised for being overly defensive, and by not being open in the early stages its credibility was badly hit. Mr Matthews, the company founder who was still the public face of the brand, did not visit the affected farm at this point and was accused by some of going into hiding. The company had lost control of the agenda, leaving the running to concerned MPs and other critics, only calling in full-scale crisis PR help relatively late in the day. Headlines such as "Matthews' empire reels as MPs go on the offensive" resulted from the criticism, and the company, according to one survey, temporarily became the least trusted consumer brand in Britain. With more openness in its media handling, the damage, mistrust and impression of disarray would have been minimised, enabling public confidence to be rebuilt more quickly.

4. Understand the importance of social media in a crisis

As I have said, social media can often be your first indicator that a crisis is brewing, which is why effective monitoring is so important. By the time a crisis hits, it is much too late to start putting social media policies into place; you need to have these running well beforehand so you can be aware of the conversations taking place, and the relevant channels open to you. This is the time to use those channels to communicate what steps you are taking to deal with the issue – to customers, and to the public at large. The world of social media is fast-evolving, so you should regularly review your plans to ensure they continue to be kept up to date. In some cases the ability for anyone, anywhere to make accusations about your company, founded or unfounded, becomes the cause of the crisis itself. For more about how this can happen and the social media aspects of crisis handling, see chapter 10.

5. Set the agenda

To repeat: if you do not set the agenda, someone else will. Think what signal you are trying to send when you give an interview, and how you can use it to achieve useful objectives. In the jargon, try to have a strong 'narrative' that clearly conveys your side of the story. Are you trying to reassure customers? Think how you can get this across this in your words and your demeanour. To appear purposeful and in control, try to provide regular updates on what steps you are taking to deal with the issue. Ensure so far as possible that you come across as a competent and well-organised organisation, taking the lead rather than finding yourself at the mercy of events. Are you organising transport, or co-operating with the health agency or trading standards officers? Tell us about it. Are you conducting a full investigation into what has occurred? Are you expecting the results of tests tomorrow? Have you ruled out a full product recall on specific advice? In all cases tell us where possible what you are doing, even if these actions may seem to you routine and obvious – they are still steps you are taking.

If you have done something wrong, admit it, unless there are specific legal obligations on you not to. You may be surprised at how much people appreciate your honesty. Organisations that are seen to have acted well in response to a crisis have on occasion actually benefited from an increase in business afterwards, often thanks to the high profile generated by the crisis.

6. Be human

If you are talking to the media in the wake of a serious incident, where there have been casualties, your priority should be to show sympathy with those affected – explanations and key messages can come afterwards. This is one of the areas we have to work hardest at with people when we are carrying out crisis media training. Individuals are usually under a lot of stress in the wake of a serious event, so that they can come over more as distracted, or self-justifying, or just highly defensive, rather than as people. If you will not apologise when on the face of it you have a lot to answer for, you may find you get ever more defensive, as the whole interview is spent trying to drag an apology out of you. You may not be able to apologise in terms of accepting responsibility for what has happened – there may be legal implications here, and you should ask for guidelines from your legal advisers as part of your crisis planning and preparation. However, lawyers being lawyers are liable to advise caution, and there have been many incidences where this has led to company spokespeople immediately losing the sympathy of the public, in some cases leading to considerable public anger.

Sometimes the reputational damage from this can be very costly, potentially outweighing any risks from saying 'sorry'. For example, in 2010 BP's then-chief executive Tony Hayward caused huge anger when he stonewalled his way through a seven-hour grilling by a US congressional panel in the wake of the Gulf of Mexico oil disaster. The approach, where he appeared unable or unwilling to answer many of the questions, refusing to admit any liability or to being aware of many key decisions leading up to the blowout, led to rising anger from members from both US political parties. The BBC reported, "As a public relations exercise for BP, the hearing was a disaster."

You have to try to find a way of showing your humanity, and expressing sympathy for a difficult or tragic situation people have found themselves in – but do choose your words carefully. In less extreme circumstances, too, you should be extra-patient, even when you are under pressure yourself and may be annoyed by the line of questioning, particularly if you find yourself having to repeatedly justify your actions to a succession of reporters and interviewers. You will look guiltier still if you are not careful. In general, you should strive to come across as reasonably as possible, even under provocation, because it is very much in your interests to do so.

Remember that the overall impression you create – particularly in radio and television interviews – is what tends to be remembered. People say things like, "Did you see that guy on the news? Wasn't he smarmy? I didn't like him." Or, if you are lucky, "I felt rather sorry for him – it was obviously very traumatic for all of them." These impressions linger long after people have forgotten the particular points you made. There is a famous quote from the writer Maya Angelou:

"I've learned that people will forget what you said, people will forget what you did, but people will never forget how you made them feel."

Six golden rules for dealing with a crisis:

1 *Integrate media into your business continuity planning; think very carefully about the practicalities, and whether you have enough people trained to handle potential media challenges and requests. The reputational damage to a business that is seen to have handled a crisis badly can exceed the other costs of the incident in terms of shareholder value.*

2 *Establish the potential categories of threat to your particular organisation, and prepare some messages that could be used if the worst happens.*

3 *Understand the importance of quick response. The way you act in the early stages of a crisis is likely to determine the media's view of your competence – or lack of it.*

4 *Understand the importance of social media in a crisis. Effective social media monitoring can give you early warning of problem issues, and social media can be a vital channel for keeping customers informed about what steps you are taking to resolve a difficult situation.*

5 *Try to set the agenda by providing regular updates and making it very clear what steps you are taking to deal with the situation, and prevent it from happening again.*

6 *Be human. If you appear too corporate, people will think you are just covering your back. Express sympathy with victims if appropriate – your key messages can come later.*

Chapter 12

Five action steps to achieve the M-factor

You really can achieve the M-factor!

Five action steps to achieve the M-factor

So what now? The best way to put the theory into practice is – by putting it into practice. You need to be able to identify the right opportunities, and be equipped to take them. Pulling together the lessons from this book, here are five action steps that will ensure you are in good shape to deal with media challenges, and where possible to turn them from threat to opportunity – in other words, ensuring you have the M-factor.

1. Use your support network

To get the M-factor most people need help. If you are a media-smart entrepreneur with a lean organisational structure and good existing media contacts, you may be happy to handle all press calls yourself, and feel you instinctively know what to say and how to get it right, in which case – great. Most people, however, especially in more corporate organisations, work within a structure. If so you should make best use of the support it provides. If you have a good internal PR function, help the team by feeding them ideas, stories and opinions, so they have plenty of material to work with. Believe me, they will appreciate the fact that you are trying to make their job easier, and this can pay dividends in terms of creating better media opportunities and relationships.

Use their knowledge and take their views seriously. They will often spot an angle in something you had not seen, or be able to warn you away from something that may create negative coverage you had not foreseen. I hear many stories from the PR people of chief executives or divisional bosses who have been expected to magically go and create positive coverage from something that really does not justify it. Senior people in an organisation can make the mistake of thinking they understand the media better than the PR professionals who deal with this sort of thing every day. Sending out swathes of dull press releases is the equivalent of crying wolf – editors will hit the 'delete' button without even opening the email, so when you really do have something interesting to say, it will probably be missed. If the advice from PR advice is to forget it, take that advice unless you really have no respect for their views, in which case do something about the PR.

Nearly all larger companies use external PR agency support even if they have a strong in-house team. This is smart as it can bring in a wider media contact base, extra creativity to come up with story angles and possible PR campaigns, not to mention strategic insight, and support in terms of warm bodies if you hit a crisis and need extra help, or need to work on a specific project. Some organisations completely outsource their PR function, although this only really works if the external agency knows your organisation extremely well and has high-level access on a continuous basis. If you feel you are not getting the right support from your existing agency, look for one with the right combination of street-smart v creative v strategic thinking for you, combined with industry knowledge and strong media contacts in your area.

As they say, "People buy people". Above all, if you are involved in the process, choose an agency team you like and respect and who you feel you will enjoy picking up the phone to. Take advice from anyone you can think of who might be able to suggest ideas as to who you should speak to, to find the agency with the best fit. Large agencies have clout and good international contacts but they can be expensive – make sure you do not fall for the old trick where they send the impressive, high-level people along for the agency pitch and then leave you with far more junior people to work with on a day-to-day basis. Smaller agencies can be nimbler, more cost-effective and less delegation-prone, and thus be a good idea so long as they have the right journalist contacts and firepower to give you full-scale assistance when you need it.

2. Identify key messages

You will never be able to give a good interview if you do not really know what you want to say. Start by making sure you are clear about your core messages; you need these ready as they could come up in any interview you give. As described in chapter 5, think through how you want to describe your business or product, how it is positioned in the market, and what its benefits are compared with the competition. If you cannot put these across clearly, do not expect a journalist to describe you accurately. Work with your PR team or external agency to ensure that you and other senior managers in the business are sending out the same signals – I am constantly amazed at how often, when I meet two or more senior people from within the same organisation, they will have radically different ways of positioning the company. Consistency is crucial. Sometimes media trainers run 'message workshops' with an organisation's top management team to help them get clarity on the strongest points they should be making, and how to convey them most effectively.

This is useful to ensure there is 'buy-in' from key participants, with a consensus emerging from those involved. Review and update these core points and supporting evidence regularly.

On top of this, think about your angle on whatever is the hot topic of the day. You want to ensure that you have something useful and relevant to offer the journalist, preferably something that differentiates you from what other people are saying, so you are adding maximum value as far as the reporters are concerned. This will make them more likely to remember to come back to you next time. If you are giving a 'responsibility' interview, however, you will need to go further and ensure you can realistically deal with whatever legitimate tough questions may be thrown at you. Your PR advisers will be of invaluable help here.

3. Get put through your paces

There is no substitute for practice. As suggested in chapter 8, if you were directing a West End play, to be performed in front of a few hundred people, I do not imagine you would hand out the scripts to the actors and then say, "Come back on opening night and make sure you have learned your lines." You would do plenty of rehearsal, particularly focusing on the bits that were tricky, or were not working well. Yet plenty of otherwise smart people will think they can just 'blag' their way through a media interview in front of a far larger audience. A good media coach or trainer is invaluable to help you bring out your points effectively, to be as interesting as possible given what you have to say, and to help you navigate the tricks and traps.

When running such sessions, I usually find that the difference in the way people perform when I give them their first interview practice, and their performance in the last one, is huge. Often the most revealing part is when I can lure them into some traps, and can then point out what awkward headlines some of their answers might have generated. Sometimes they are all too aware they have got themselves into trouble; on other occasions they do not even realise. Having learned their lesson, they are resolved not to make the same mistakes again, and are much more likely to be able to avoid the booby-traps next time.

If possible, choose a media trainer who is highly experienced, and informed about your subject, but not too informed – they need to have enough distance to ensure they are approaching the interview from an external perspective (like most journalists), not from that of an 'insider'. Any ex-journalist can give you a tough time in an interview; the real skill comes in being able to immediately feedback in a constructive way how you could have done it differently and achieved a better result. Poor media training will make you look and sound corporate and pushy, instead of helping you to draw out the points so you can put them across as effectively as possible.

4. Identify your target media

Be clear about the people you would like to influence and communicate with via the media – is it customers, clients, regulators, local people? If you do not already know, find out what publications they read, or which radio/television channels or individual journalists are the most influential. Focus your media energies on building up relationships with these where possible, so you can maximise impact; you may sometimes be surprised. Do not focus only on gossipy trade press, if your potential customers are reading different publications entirely. Think about what topics those publications tend to write about, and what they are likely to be interested in, and then think how you could be useful to them. A good relationship built up in this way can generate steady coverage. If you have something interesting to say, it is much easier to pick up the phone to a reporter and say, "I wondered if you'd be interested in this?" if you already know them. This level of contact may also stand you in good stead if you hit problems – at least there is a pre-existing relationship there, and they are more likely to give you fair coverage or the benefit of the doubt.

The connection can be made initially by you offering them relevant material; at other times, your PR advisers may recommend relationship-building lunches or social events. However, bear in mind that reporters rarely have time for that sort of thing unless they really do think there will be something in it for them in terms of content. Even at a 'getting-to-know-you' lunch with a key journalist, you should have an agenda, with something you think could make a story. Applying M-factor principles you should make it a fun, relaxing occasion if possible so the reporter comes away liking you – but also thinking it was worth it in terms of giving him or her industry insight, quote-worth views or a specific news story.

Many trade publications will accept 'placed articles' if you can make them interesting and relevant for their readers – it is free material for them. Your PR advisers should know what opportunities exist in your sector. However, these cannot just be a company or product plug – apply the same principles of having something useful and interesting to say first of all, and then you can weave your own messages in as appropriate. Always – always – give what you have written to someone else to read through first; sometimes you can miss obvious gaffes that others will spot immediately. If you are not a natural writer, jot down the key points and get someone better suited to the job to turn it into flowing prose.

Other opportunities may come with a price tag attached. It would be nice to think that media coverage depends entirely on merit; however, some trade journals operate on the basis that your company needs to buy some advertising to help support the publication before they will support you by giving coverage. Many go a step further and take 'advertorial', or paid-for editorial coverage, which is clearly marked as such. These options may be of value on occasions, although usually the publications that are taken most seriously are the ones that keep advertising and editorial as separate as possible. Having said that, a healthy media needs support from advertisers, otherwise it will wither and die, so this type of financial support can certainly generate goodwill and mean you are given more of a shot than your opposite number from a company that does not advertise. A further profile-raising opportunity can come from sponsoring the industry awards that are run by some publications, which can provide another route to creating media links that could turn into coverage.

5. Watch what others do

Learn what you can from the way others play the media. Who already has the M-factor in your sector, and what can you learn from them? Do they come up with better quotes, with better information, or is their success simply down to the fact that they are willing to turn up or take the call? You have to be willing to put yourself about a bit; it may mean cancelling an engagement or getting up unconscionably early in the morning to get out and do a radio interview. You will have to make a judgment call each time as to whether it is worth it – but from years of working in radio and television, I know producers really remember the people who got them out of a hole by being willing to fill an interview slot when they could not find anyone else at short notice. That is how certain people have become such frequent commentators – simply by reliably delivering value to the audience, and by being willing to devote the time to it, when others were busy or slow to return calls. If your topic is not of interest to the wider market, you can still achieve the M-factor in your own sector, which is all that matters if that is what will help you raise presence and demonstrate leadership with your target market.

Think about what are the current hot issues in your sector are, and ensure you have some relevant views on these that you are willing to share. Then you are 'oven-ready' when the media opportunity comes up, rather than having to go away for hours to think what you want to say. Is there a bandwagon that you can jump on? Some people have achieved a considerable profile by firing off emails to their media list commenting on everything from tax announcements to new legislative proposals – "AcmeCo warns of threat to widget industry." These may be completely ignored, or may be meat and drink to the publication with space to fill. You will not know until you try.

Watch television and listen to the radio with a more knowledgeable eye and ear. Look out for the people who impress you – what are they doing, and could you be doing the same? Is it their style, demeanour, passion, warmth, articulacy? What about those people that annoy you? Check with those around you that you do not sometimes make the same mistakes. Once you have the M-factor you will be attuned to these things, picking up ideas and pointers without even thinking about it.

Embrace the media – they will change and mutate, but they aren't going away. If you have tough issues, you need to get media-savvy. If you have good, fun stuff to talk about, or if you want to position yourself as a leader in your field, you have fantastic opportunities in front of you – take them.

Five action steps:

1 *Use your support network. Take PR advice seriously; help your PRs to help you to build good media relationships, by feeding them with story ideas and information when you can, and by responding quickly to media enquiries.*

2 *Identify your key messages. Try to have some interesting views, as well as thinking about how you can most effectively position yourself in your industry; if you do not bang your own drum, no one else will do it for you.*

3 *Get put through your paces. Ensure you have high-quality media training to help you come across well, rather than as corporate and pushy.*

4 *Identify your target media. Be clear about who you want to communicate with and influence, and try to build relationships with the key publications they read.*

5 *Watch what others do. Think who already has the M-factor in related sectors – what can you learn from them? Look out for issues already of interest to the media that you might be able to comment on. Embrace the media – they aren't going away.*

What they say about the M-factor

This book is a goldmine of information for PR practitioners, as well as any business leader who wants to be able to work effectively with the media, in good times or bad. Tom has put many of my clients through training sessions over the years and really knows his stuff!

Gay Collins,
Executive Chairman, MHP Communications

In today's fast moving 24/7 media world, being confident with the press is an essential business skill and something we all need to be good at. Tom Maddocks is a master of his art and this fabulous little book is full of great advice and life saving do's and don'ts. The M-factor is essential reading for those at the beginning of their management career, equally it will prove an invaluable refresher for experienced business managers who need to pep up their media skills.

Fiona Harris,
Managing Director Quill PR

The media can be a threat or an opportunity, depending on how you treat them. If you want to understand how to get the media on-side, in good times or bad, this book is a good place to start!

Sir Stuart Rose,
former Chairman and Chief Executive, Marks & Spencer plc

About the author

Tom Maddocks is the founder and Course Director of Media Training Associates, which works with spokespeople from a variety of organisations, helping them take advantage of media opportunities. Recognised as one of the UK's leading media and presentation skills coaches, he has been quoted in the Independent, Sunday Times, Financial Times, PR Week and others. Tom has worked extensively for BBC Radio and Television and Channel Four, including a five-year stint as a reporter on BBC2's The Money Programme.

For more guidance and videos from Tom, information on courses and to sign up for his free monthly media and presentation tips newsletter, go to
www.mediatrainingassociates.co.uk

Notes

Notes

Notes

Notes

Notes